T0162805

IGUANAS ON MY ROOF

Funny, Sad, and Scary OVERSEAS ADVENTURES of a Foreign Service Family in Third-World Countries during the Vietnam War and Watergate Era

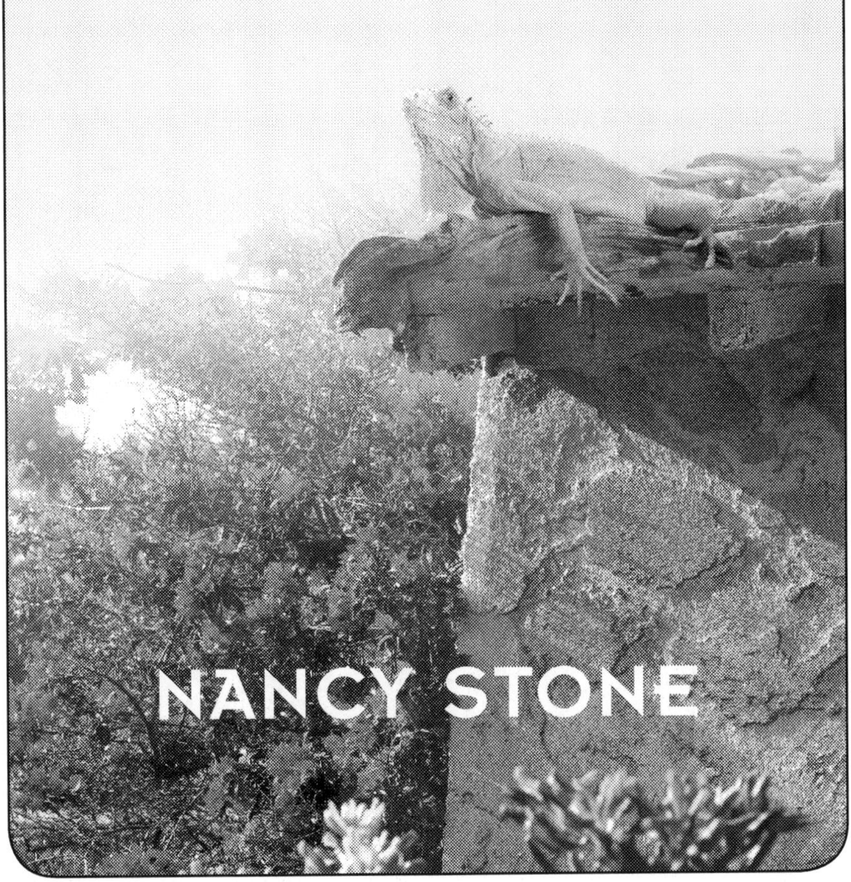

NANCY STONE

WestBow Press books may be ordered through booksellers or by contacting:

WestBow Press
A Division of Thomas Nelson & Zondervan
1663 Liberty Drive
Bloomington, IN 47403
www.westbowpress.com
1 (866) 928-1240

ISBN: 978-1-4908-2322-5 (sc)
ISBN: 978-1-4908-2323-2 (hc)
ISBN: 978-1-4908-2321-8 (e)

Library of Congress Control Number: 2014901165

Printed in the United States of America.

WestBow Press rev. date: 1/29/2014

IGUANA STEW

Serves ~~6~~ ~~8~~ 4

(Who knows? Most people won't eat it.)

1 large iguana
1 tsp. salt
3 peeled and sliced potatoes
1 large sliced onion
1 cup lima beans
1 cup canned tomatoes
1 tbsp. sugar
1 cup frozen corn
1 tbsp. ketchup or Worcestershire Sauce
1/4 cup butter

Cut iguana meat into small pieces.
Place meat in a large pot with enough water to cover.
Bring to a boil, add salt, and simmer for 45 minutes.
Add potatoes, onion, lima beans, tomatoes, and sugar.
Cover and simmer for 30 minutes.
Add corn and simmer for 10 minutes.
Add ketchup or Worcestershire Sauce if desired.
Add butter and stir well.

Thank you to my husband who had to live for months with a wife constantly in front of her computer and to my children who helped me remember.

CHAPTER SUMMARIES

1. Introduction 1
   An introduction to my family and life at diplomatic missions in underdeveloped countries.

2. Why We Did It 5
   My husband, Al, wanted to make a difference in the lives of people in distress. He joined the Foreign Service.

3. Getting Ready to Go 7
   Al was sent to Saigon. I was left alone with five children to complete a long list of etceteras. I only had to call the police once.

MANILA, PHILIPPINES

4. A New Way of Life 13
   With my husband a thousand miles away, I had to manage a household of servants and be Miss Manners at Embassy functions.

5. Not Exactly the US Post Office 21
   There was a steady stream of maids delivering letters to hand-carry back to Saigon.

6. Protocol and Etiquette 21
   Formal "Official Calls" were required. There were a few mishaps along the way.

7. The American School 23
   School in third-world countries from the kid's point of view.

8. Grocery Shopping 101-103 25
It was intimidating to have an armed guard posted at the end of the aisle at the grocery store.

9. Just Like a Date 27
The hotel gave me early access on the days my husband arrived to set up a "can you top this" evening.

10. Language and Culture 28
Tradition and superstition had to be respected.

11. My Friend, the Colonel 30
The Colonel invited me to the elaborate wedding for his son.

12. It Wasn't the Flu 34
Our son lost nearly one-third of his body weight before we could get him to reliable medical care over a road terrorized by Philippine guerrillas.

13. Black Magic Exists 38
Our maids were cursed by a black magic charm.

14. Over the Rapids with Grandma 39
Why I thought it was a good idea to take my Mother and five kids over dangerous rapids to Pagsanjan Falls in hollowed out logs, I don't know.

15. Baguio Guest House 41
The main entrance road ran between the holes on the golf course—and the flying golf balls.

16. Nothing Like the Brochure 43
The "facilities" was a bathroom of corrugated metal sheets propped up on poles in the sand.

17. Memories on the Bataan Peninsula and Corregidor Island 45
Our guide said the dark stains in the stones on the beach were blood.

SAIGON, VIETNAM

18. The Vietnamese Experience 49
To get to the refugee camps, Al flew low over the jungle to keep from being shot down.

19. Language and Culture 52
French influence was everywhere. Whole families piled onto a single motorcycle.

20. Protocol and Etiquette 54
Ambassador Laise was kind enough to ignore my rubber flip flops at her reception.

21. You Buy Me Saigon Tea? 55
Bar girls took me on a whirlwind day excursion to buy silk.

MANILA, PHILIPPINES TO LAGOS, NIGERIA

22. Bangkok, Thailand 61
Bangkok was a fairyland of temples, gold Buddhas, and crowded waterways.

23. Mumbai, India 65
Families were living on the sidewalks. An ox-cart carried away the dead.

24. Tel Aviv, Israel 68
They wouldn't let us off the plane because someone exploded a bomb.

25. Athens, Greece and Rome, Italy 69
We made minestrone in a country restaurant. Our cat became an illegal immigrant.

LAGOS, NIGERIA

26. A New Way of Life 75
The kids were escorted to school by a guard armed with an M2 carbine rifle.

27. What Daddy did at his Nigerian Office 82
Al set up health programs where children often die before the age of three months.

28. Language and Culture 84
Our cook cut his own whip and handed it to Al, expecting a beating.

29. Grocery Shopping 104-106 87
Nigeria had few goods available and sanitation was not a word in their dictionary.

30. Black Magic Again 89
Juju charms protected our house at night.

31. Stranded at Tarkwa Bay 90
It is hard to describe the isolation we felt with only the African jungle and sand.

32. Now You See Them, Then You Don't 93
An alert son saw our twenty-one suitcases being loaded onto a private truck at the airport.

WASHINGTON DC

33. What Daddy did at his DC Office 99
People in Bangladesh had something to eat because Al found ways to ship food to them.

34. DC Does its own Thing 100
Watergate needs no explanation. State Department functions are not as reported in the newspapers.

FROM DC TO MANAGUA, NICARAGUA

35. Southward Ho 107
We pulled a fourteen-foot travel trailer through detours in corn fields and took turns watching for livestock on the road.

MANAGUA, NICARAGUA

36. What Daddy did at his Nicaraguense Office 115
Managua looked like a bombed city in World War II when we arrived.

37. A New Way of Life 119
My high school Spanish didn't make the grade.

38. Grocery Shopping 107-110 123
The few stores that survived the earthquake relocated in homes in outlying areas.

39. Protocol and Etiquette 124
I wish my dog hadn't been there to greet the wife of the Chief of Mission.

40. Language and Culture 126
When it became difficult to communicate at functions, I took refuge in the bathroom.

41. The American School 129
There weren't enough classrooms in the temporary chicken-coop style buildings.

42. Not Your Usual Ministry Meeting 131
My Spanish caused the cook to serve sandwiches of roast beef nestled in peanut butter and jelly to the Ministers of the Nicaraguense government.

43. The Dreadful Terremoto (Earthquake) 133
Our maid was paralyzed with fear. I will never forget the terror in her eyes.

44. Call a Marine... 135
The formal Marine Corps Ball was the social highlight of the year. The Marines were our Boy Scout leaders. Some of what they taught was not in the Scout Manual.

45. Turtle Eggs and HueHuete Beach..................................... 138
We had to cross a river with no bridge with our travel trailer. Turtle-egg hunting was a treat.

46. Iguanas on my Roof 140
Iguanas sounded like five-hundred pound dragons on our metal roof.

47. Thanksgiving—Nicaraguense Style.................................. 142
Several families sat in candle light under a carport and sang.

48. Head Him Off at the Pass 144
In Panama, a purse snatcher broke my thumb. We smuggled two kids into Nicaragua.

49. Not So Perfect End to a Perfect Evening........................... 149
Men armed with M2 carbines stopped our car. Terrorists were holding hostages.

50. So Many Volcanoes.. 151
We were able to lie down on the edge of a volcano and watch the lava surge toward us.

51. A Big Mistake 154
Our son went on a quick ride with friends and was arrested on drug charges.

WE WENT BACK HOME

52. The End of the Story 161
Three of our five children lived in the States. We decided to join them.

INTRODUCTION

My husband's job in the Foreign Service was to follow wars and disasters around the world. My job was to follow him into an unfamiliar world that was exciting and challenging.

Would I have changed anything? No.

Why? First, we were right in the middle of the often befuddling process we call "government," so we better understood that the precious freedoms in the United States had to be fiercely protected. Second, our five children grew up independent, confident, and not easily intimidated. Third, we learned that good friends could be found in any culture. Fourth, we were privileged to meet many people who were making decisions that changed the world.

It was exciting, always interesting, certainly challenging, and because we were so far away from family and friends, we learned to trust in and depend on each other—a very special gift. To complete the picture, there was a wonderful feeling of satisfaction from knowing we benefitted a country and its people by being there.

Besides, I had help with the housework and laundry, did very little cooking, and didn't pull a single weed. With a family of seven, I loved it. Even though there were a few "inconveniences" like iguanas on the roof, I had found a home in the Foreign Service.

Movie version: The chartered plane glides to a stop. The door opens and a dashing Foreign Service officer appears in the bright sun. Next to him, draped in fur, is his beautiful wife. Their Russian Wolfhound is close behind. The Ambassador waits at the bottom of the stairs to welcome them to an exciting, sophisticated world capital. The beautiful people have a beautiful life that is a whirlwind of intrigue, elegant dinner parties, and fancy balls. They hobnob with presidents and dignitaries from all over the world.

My version: Pan Am was always our host for the flight. The door opened and we drowned in the humidity. We were rumpled from hours of travel and the Embassy aide who met us at the airport was definitely not the Ambassador.

We had to live for three months with what we could carry, so we always crammed as much as we could in our luggage. It took a long time to get through Customs with five kids and twenty-one suitcases. Throw in a cranky cat and I think you get the picture.

As for the sophisticated capitals, beginning in 1968, the State Department sent us to unsophisticated Vietnam, Nigeria, and Nicaragua with a stopover in Washington DC. Even so, the diplomats, fancy balls, and elegant dinners were a way of life. It was an extraordinary adventure.

I was asked many times to write about circling the globe with five children. Nearly thirty years later, my daughter made me promise to email my children one story each week. I pretended they were sitting in front of me and let the words spill out. As they added comments, it became a fun family project. This book is the result.

Let me introduce my family. My husband's name is Al (Jr.). Our children are Butch (Al III), who is the eldest, then Jim, Janice, Kenny, and Eric. When we left the United States they ranged in age from twelve years to eighteen months. We were away for eight years.

Stone Family
Butch (Al III), Jim, Nancy, Al, Eric, Janice, Kenny
Bombay (Mumbai) India 1970

WHY WE DID IT

It all started when my husband decided to save the people of Mexico.

During the drought in 1959, Al worked as a railroad brakeman. He saw firsthand the swarms of dehydrated and starving Mexicans with swollen tongues who regularly overpowered and boarded the trains that traveled through the Mexican desert and in and out of the southwestern United States. They were desperate and dangerous. Their last hope was to illegally enter the United States. Al was determined to help Mexico help them.

With only a high school diploma and deadly serious about his decision, Al found a new job with flexible hours and enrolled in college. His goal was to join the Foreign Service. Five years later, he held a dual degree in Accounting and Economics with a Latin American emphasis. I worked, took care of our four children, and typed all his homework on a tiny portable typewriter. I received an honorary degree for being a good sport.

It took another four years, but Al eventually applied and was accepted by the US Department of State, an extremely difficult and demanding process. He resigned his job in 1968 as Administrator with the Marin County Welfare Department in California and accepted the position of Program Officer with USAID (US Agency for International Development). This agency works to improve the lives of people living in underdeveloped countries.

In typical government fashion, his knowledge of the economy, culture, and language of Latin America was ignored. His first assignment was not Mexico, but Saigon. There he was to coordinate the efforts of the United States government and thirty-three relief agencies such as CARE, Catholic Relief, OXFAM, and World Vision. These formed a major part of the Vietnamese Refugee Program. Geographically, if Saigon had been any farther away from Mexico, he would be coming back around the globe on the other side.

People were shooting at each other in Vietnam so joining him was not an option. Al did some research and found that USAID offered three safe-haven Posts to the families of men and women working in Vietnam. One was in Thailand, another was in Taiwan, and a third in the Republic of the Philippines. We couldn't take advantage of any of these Posts until there was an opening. Al was gone six months before housing was offered to us in the Philippines. We took it.

GETTING READY TO GO

Al left for three months of language training in Washington DC. That left me with the now five children and the responsibility to prepare for the move. Our next door neighbor had been in the Philippines during his tour in the Navy. He began telling me horror stories about dead bodies in the back yard, security walls with embedded glass around homes, and gruesome crimes. He had me terrified, but my Mother convinced me the move was a wonderful opportunity that we shouldn't miss. She was right, although I fully expected to be machine-gunned from behind a palm tree upon arrival in Manila.

We were given a date only a few short weeks away and there was a ridiculously long "To Do List." I had to hire an agent to manage the rental of the house. The Philippine government would not allow us to bring a car, so I had to sell mine. We were in the middle of some house remodeling. Everyone needed a full medical examination and an extraordinarily long list of inoculations. Janice, Jim and Butch had to be tested in order to enter the American School. We needed passports and tickets.

> **I needed a clearance:** I attended classes from 7:00 to 10:00 three nights a week at College of Marin about thirty miles away. On the way home one evening I noticed a car that turned each time I did. As I drove into my cul-de-sac, it moved into an unlit parking lot opposite my street. The headlights went dark.
>
> My neighbor crossed the street to stay with my kids while I drove the baby-sitter home. The car edged in behind me to and from the sitter's, then returned to the parking lot. There was no cell phone in those days. I had to wait until I got home to call police. It seemed a long walk from the drive-way to the front door.

> We turned off the house lights and watched from the kitchen window. The car, headlights off, slowly crept from the parking lot to my curb. With five children and a neighbor in the house, I remember wishing I had a gun.
>
> The police officer forced the man out of his car and made him put his hands on the fender, but stepped back when the man waved something. The "something" was FBI identification. The agent was upset, I was upset, and the police officer was not happy about a false alarm. Hopefully, the agent learned a lesson on how to investigate a clearance without scaring someone to death.

Al had taken out the hall closet in order to enlarge the kitchen, so the tile floor had to be extended. The piano had cracked some tiles in the family room. I wasted days trying to find matching asphalt tile and a contractor to replace them. I gave up and learned how to iron the floor to take up old tiles and lay new ones.

I called every real estate office in town and finally found an agent to manage the house rental that had good referrals and didn't charge outlandish fees. I said a prayer and signed a two-year contract.

I didn't know how to handle test drives to sell the car. (Should I let someone drive off with my car or should I get in the car with a stranger?) Thank Heaven a friend needed a car and would wait to take possession until the day we left.

Because we were State Department, we could use military facilities. Al held the equivalent rank of full Colonel which allowed us special privileges. We made twenty-one trips to (the now closed) Hamilton Air Force Base for inoculations. The older children could receive some of the nine different inoculations in one dose. The younger ones had to have the same inoculation in two doses. Eric was eighteen-months old and had to have them in three. Of course, everyone had sore arms, ran fevers and got cranky—including me.

We had our passport pictures taken at Hamilton as well.

> **Lesson learned:** Not knowing any better, I let them put Eric, Kenny and me on one passport. It created a horrible problem when I wanted to go to Vietnam later. If I took the one combined passport with me, it left the two of them outside of the United States with no passport of their own. The Embassy later made new ones for each of the boys.

It was summer and most schools were closed, but after calling every school in the phone book, I managed to find testing agencies that gave the exams required to enter the Philippine American School. Of course, all were on different days.

I couldn't get an appointment for medical exams at Hamilton before my deadline. I found a medical office at an obscure base on the State Department list that was about thirty miles away. Poor Butch, the only date available for exams was on his birthday. We drove to the facility, pulling off onto a tiny, narrow road. It dead-ended at a military gate. I couldn't see anyone so I slowly pulled in through the gate. The old baby-blue Chevy station wagon crammed with five kids must have looked threatening because I heard the loud crack of a shot and someone yelling, "Halt!" The guard wasn't the least bit interested in my explanation. A jeep with armed men came out of nowhere and escorted us to a medical office in a Quonset hut. We got the exams, but found there was no x-ray machine. That meant I had to schedule another trip to Hamilton for x-rays. I never did learn what they did at that base.

Al came home for a few days before he left for Vietnam. I felt achy and terrible the whole time he was there, but didn't want to take the time away from our visit to see a doctor. I drove him to the airport. I felt so sick that I just dropped him at the door pretending it would be too hard to say good-bye if I went inside. I remember laying my head against the car window most of the way home. The next day my doctor told me I had to be hospitalized immediately with a serious kidney infection.

Great. Al had just gone and I had five kids with no help. My Mother and sister lived about seventy-five miles away and couldn't get away from work. Two of my neighbors said they could "check" on the kids. To this day, I don't know exactly what that meant. I had a baby only eighteen months old.

Just when I thought things couldn't get worse, I turned on the hospital television to see a massive earthquake in Tokyo. There was image after image of crumpled buildings. Al was there on a layover. I tried to track him through the State Department. They weren't any help. I just had to wait until I heard from him.

I shouldn't have watched the television news. The Tet Offensive in Saigon was on every channel. Did Al survive the Tokyo earthquake just to die in Saigon? That did it. My children were home alone with little or no supervision and my husband was somewhere between an earthquake and a Viet Cong invasion. The medication the doctors were giving me made me throw up. I found my clothes and went home.

Several agonizing days passed. The phone would ring, but it wasn't Al. Finally, he called from the Embassy to tell me he had arrived safely. I bombarded him with questions and my situation all at the same time. When he could interrupt, he told me he had flown on to Hong Kong before the earthquake, but had met Tet head-on. Not a good start with USAID.

In the meantime, I was still working on the "To Do List." State Department instructions were to sort all our belongings four ways. Sort One was for the trip. We were allowed forty-pounds and a carry-on per person. What we brought with us had to last at least three months until the air freight would arrive. Sort Two was for air freight. Sort Three was the surface shipment. Sort Four was for storage.

Where do you put all the different things while you try to live in a sixteen-hundred square-foot house with five children? Some of these piles eventually filled half a room. We all kept pulling things we needed out of each pile.

It seemed like a simple concept, but the packers and movers couldn't seem to understand which pile went where. First, the packers mixed everything up. Then the movers sent things to the wrong place. It might have been easier if they hadn't also packed my signs that said Travel, Storage, Air Freight, and Surface Freight.

We finally reached the day before our 10:00 p.m. flight out of San Francisco. Our plane tickets, mailed from DC, were nowhere to be found. After a million phone calls, the State Department located them at 4:00 o'clock. They were in the main post office in downtown San Francisco over an hour away. The post office closed at 5:00. A grouchy postman met us at the back gate after hours.

My Mother drove us to the airport the next evening. Did you know that seven people and eighteen suitcases could be crammed into a 1964 Pontiac sedan? Atop the suitcases, the kid's heads touched the roof. We had to slow down over bumps.

An aunt and uncle met us at the gate to say good-bye. (In saner days you could walk a passenger to the boarding gate.) My sister and her husband were supposed to be there, but were late. We couldn't wait for them, so I boarded the plane. I was getting everyone settled when my sister appeared in the aisle with Eric. She was allowed on the plane to say good-by and to bring my youngest child aboard. I had left him at the gate in all the hugging and crying and saying good-bye. This comes under the heading of "things you wish you hadn't done."

I thought I could finally relax, but no ...

We taxied out to the runway. The plane suddenly braked. It shuddered and groaned to a stop. The Captain assured us that everything was fine as we taxied somewhere and sat in the dark. The plane took off again. It braked a second time. I kept wondering if we going to slide into San Francisco Bay. I had five children on that plane. Now, I just wanted to get out of there. The stewardess (at one time you could reveal the sex of the flight attendant) told me to sit down.

We finally got off the ground on the third try—three hours later. Our twenty-one hour flight turned into twenty-four hours. We followed darkness around the globe. It was a kind of blessing as everyone slept a good part of time.

Al was waiting for me at the airport in Manila, so everything was going to be okay.

MANILA, PHILIPPINES

August 1968 to February 1970

My husband was living and working in a war zone. I was on my own with five children at my first Post.

A NEW WAY OF LIFE

Alone with five children in a foreign culture was pretty scary at first. After the first few weeks though with a cook, maid, nanny, part-time gardener, and seamstress, I felt I had found a home in the Foreign Service. I didn't have to dust and mop, wash and iron, mow the grass, pull weeds, and rarely had to cook.

Along with the great benefits, came responsibilities. All of these had to be met with no car for the first six months and no phone at all. I soon found that although I wasn't doing the work, I was now running a household with employees who had personal problems, complaints, needed instruction, and a paycheck. It is like running a company, but you are President, Vice President, Human Resources, Payroll, Benefits, and Legal all rolled into one.

Menus and grocery lists had to be planned with the cook. Instructions for each girl had to be made clear each day. If you were lucky, the cook, who was always in charge, could direct the other girls.

For six months, a trip to the grocery store or anywhere was by taxi. With no phone, you had to walk until you found one and carry whatever you needed with you. Philippine taxis were about the size of the front seat of your Chevy. If the kids were with me, everyone sat under someone or on their lap.

Our first maids were wonderful. Our house was large with four bedrooms and four bathrooms—a lot to care for. I remember looking in the drawer of my dressing table and all my curlers were standing on end and matched to size. I was impressed.

It was hard not to make the bed, help clear the table, or grab a dish cloth in the kitchen. When I took the trash to the curb where someone might see me, they jointly sat me down and complained that I kept doing things that they considered their job. They were afraid people would think they were bad employees. I had a lot to learn.

Blessing or worry? One of the best ways to teach kids responsibility is to assign them chores. The chores usually done in an American home were done here by maids. I had to be creative.

Nettie, our cook, made the best cinnamon rolls in the world. My bedroom had a button on the wall above the bed that rang in the kitchen. When Al was home, I would reach up and push the button before we got out of bed. Nettie would come in with cinnamon rolls fresh out of the oven and piping hot coffee. Life was good.

Nahty was our lavendera (laundry maid). She was studying accounting at the University of Santa Tomas in Quezon City. We tried to help her as much as we could with tuition, books, and other costs. We were lucky to have Delia who helped with the kids and cleaned. All of them helped each other. I thought it was interesting that Nettie had her own maid at home.

Public education from first to sixth grade is free and mandatory in the Philippines. This was a gift from the US and General MacArthur after World War II. It made a huge difference in working with my staff. My girls could read so I could leave written instructions. They could read labels and directions on a package. Later, in other countries, I learned that there was a definite problem where there was no education, lots of superstition, and prejudices.

Although everyone had the opportunity for education, there weren't enough jobs. Americans had a reputation for paying high wages, so working for an American was preferred. The lifeguard at the pool at Seafront, our little PX (military store), had a college degree. I was criticized by several Filipinas for paying more to our staff because it made it harder for them to hire at the "going" local rates.

Nettie left us and Dina took her place. She had a degree in Home Economics and knew more about many things than I did. She didn't let her ten little stubs for fingers stop her from slicing vegetables in the kitchen or picking up the heavy wooden cases of liter bottles of soda pop we had delivered regularly. Delia stayed with us until we left. Nahty graduated and left.

The Philippine government would not allow us to bring a car into the country, but we could wait until an Embassy family was leaving and buy from them. The first opportunity came after six months. I bought a family's Chevy Impala and hired their maid, Anita. While she was working for us, my grandmother's platinum watch and platinum ring with a ruby and diamonds disappeared. Knowing what I know now, I would not have taken that precious jewelry overseas in the first place. I had to fire her.

We had a gardener, even though there wasn't very much garden. Land was at a premium. Our house was very large and within a few feet of a wall which was imbedded with jagged glass. Wages were so low and temperatures and humidity were so high that the gardener was not really a luxury even though it only took an hour or so a week to maintain the yard.

Remie, the seamstress, came one day a week. She made her own patterns from a catalog. It was wonderful to have custom clothing, but it also meant that each Tuesday I had to be sure

I had projects and fabric with matching thread ready for her. The material had to be soaked in salt water and then washed and ironed ahead of time to set the colors. She could make two shirts or one dress in a day.

Because we were in the tropics, most of the clothes were made of cotton. Remie made dresses for Janice and me and shirts for Al and the boys. Why have a seamstress? Clothes for the kids were available, but unless you were tiny, men and women's clothing in the stores were too small. The beautiful hand-embroidered fabrics came in pre-cut lengths of three meters. That was fine if you were small like most of the Filipinas, but for an American, it was pretty skimpy. The hand sewn dresses were almost always made the same. The embroidery would be down the front and a scatter pattern down the zippered back. There usually wasn't enough fabric for a collar or sleeves.

Dresses were still preferred in those days. Remie came up with a solution to the high winds. She made pantaloons of very delicate batiste with lace trim. They were pretty and cool and if the wind blew my dress too high, I would just show off my fancy pantaloons. It wasn't long before she was making them for my friends.

As soon as we had a car, I hired Macario to drive one day a week. This was not a luxury either. In most places you really did not want to leave your car unattended as it would be stripped when you returned. Macario would take me, and often one or two of my friends, on errands. He would stay with the car. If you had an accident, it was a much better if you were not the driver.

One of our favorite places was a bakery in Chinatown that made wonderful almond cookies. It became known that we went once a week. We actually started taking orders to fill from other Embassy wives. Chinatown was a great place to shop, but pretty scary. Horse-drawn carriages called calesas were everywhere. The calesa looked like the hansom cabs in a Sherlock Holmes movie—right down to the lanterns swinging on either side. The streets were narrow and incredibly crowded. Even Macario wouldn't brave them. He would drop us off and park nearby, watching for us to appear at the curb.

I admit it was fun having a driver. At the airport, and many restaurants and hotels, there was a man or even a booth on the curb with a loud speaker or microphone. You were dropped off at the curb. When you were ready to leave, "Driver Macario" would be announced and your driver would pick you up. It was like valet parking, only you got to keep the driver. When my Mother came to visit us, I hired Macario for the week. She got a big kick out of being driven around in the back seat—even though she was in a Chevrolet with no air conditioning.

We found that the Sheraton Hotel spa closed to the public at 10:00 each night. After that hour, it could be rented for private parties. Several times some friends and I got together for a sauna bath, pressure shower, and massage. Macario drove on those nights.

The average wage for a maid was about thirty dollars a month plus a rice allowance. The rice allowance was either the promise to keep rice on hand, usually a 50-pound bag, or an equivalent amount of money. Remie, Macario and the gardener earned two dollars and fifty cents, plus lunch, per day. You were expected to provide uniforms and sleeping quarters for the maids. They usually rotated Sundays and holidays off. Sometimes you would be alone on a Sunday and have to cook lunch for the gardener or driver.

The air-conditioning allowance from the Embassy was one air-conditioning unit per bedroom. As a result, the living room, dining room, kitchen, and maid's quarters, could be very uncomfortable. Unless it was totally inappropriate, almost everyone entertained in the master bedroom. It was usually large enough to set up a love seat and a few chairs in a conversation corner.

The maids' quarters had no hot water in their shower. In fact, neither did most of the houses. I tried without success to get the Embassy to install hot water for them. Electricity and water seemed a bad combination to me, but believe it or not, there was an electric shower head heating the shower water of many homes. The Embassy facility staff actually laughed and razzed me about the request. I didn't think it was funny.

If an employee became pregnant or ill, you became the health benefit. One of our maids contracted hepatitis and was hospitalized. The hospital gives the family prescriptions which they fill at an outside pharmacy. The hospital will then administer the medications. Meals were also provided by the family. If you are hospitalized and have no help, you are in big trouble. Al and I supplied most of our maid's needs. Another of our maids would deliver food and medications each day by taxi. We did find one advantage to seeing the actual prescriptions. Al happened to be in-country (Manila) and discovered one prescription for a medication that could have killed her. He was able to prevent a disaster.

> **Note:** The term "in-country" is common usage in the Foreign Service. It is the country you are in at the time you are speaking.

Because she had a contagious disease, we had to notify the Embassy. Unfortunately, this occurred very shortly after Christmas when there were more men in-country from Vietnam than at any other time. It was also one of the few times that families tried to get together. That meant we exposed a majority of the Saigon families posted in Manila to the disease.

The Embassy immediately notified everyone they needed a gamma globulin shot for protection. There wasn't enough serum to go around so they borrowed from other countries. We weren't exactly the most popular family for awhile.

If you knew the name of a medication you could buy it at any drugstore without a prescription. That has a lot of advantages. There are also a few disadvantages. The local drug stores were refilling birth control pill containers with their own version of the contraception pill. Several women added new members to their families before that was known. After that, we asked someone from the States to fill our prescriptions. The pills from the States became a precious commodity.

Our husbands visited from Vietnam for a few days every six weeks. Women, dealing with cycles as they do, wanted to be free to thoroughly enjoy the visits with their husbands in every way. So—if your husband was coming in-country at an inconvenient time in your cycle, you could borrow a few pills to extend the cycle. You can see that it would be important to pay back the pills. We had an elaborate accounting system in place in order to know who owed who how many pills and when. It is a wonder we didn't all get cancer or something.

Mosquitoes were a way of life. Spray trucks drove the streets and sprayed the sidewalks and the adjacent bushes. If you happened to be walking down the street, you got sprayed as well. The kids confessed years later that they followed the trucks on their bikes. That may explain times they felt sick with no obvious explanation. Heaven knows what kind of poison they were spraying. The industry is not regulated.

Note: A jar of Vicks VapoRub ointment sat on nearly every night table to take the itch away from a mosquito bite. The "fragrance" of mentholated Vicks was everywhere.

Worms were dangerous. They burrow under the skin of a bare foot and work their way into your system. Our kids were not allowed to go barefoot for eight years.

Every household had to deal with roaches. They were big enough to carry our Stateside roaches home for a snack. We were afraid to have the house sprayed by a commercial company because no one could tell us what poisons they used. Boric acid was our solution to the problem. Drugstores sold it by the pound in paper bags. The bugs couldn't digest it so we spread the stuff under shelf paper and around outside doors. The bugs helped by carrying it back to the nest.

Checks were accepted at the Embassy PX, but cash was king everywhere else. The Embassy provided an office where we could cash a Stateside check and receive pesos or a minimum number of dollars. Many trips were made.

One terrifying trip put me right in the middle of a political demonstration at the Embassy gate. There were about twenty men milling around the wrought iron fence some fifty feet away from the guard post. I stopped to show my identification. Suddenly, there were faces in every window. I felt the car tilting to the left, then rocking to the right and back again. With no air-conditioning, my windows were rolled down and an open invitation to reach inside. Beyond the faces in my windshield, I could see three Marines pointing loaded guns to thin out the crowd and make a path for me through the gate to safety. I put my foot on the gas pedal and prayed that I wouldn't run over someone as I moved forward. Thank God for Marines.

You had to plan ahead for one currency or the other any time you shopped, rode in a taxi, ate out, went to a movie, took the kids to the pool, or met your payroll. It was not safe to carry cash, but I couldn't think of a place to hide it. Maids were in every part of my home. I finally hit on a solution that worked over the many years we were overseas. I bought a new douche bag in a box. I threw out the douche bag and hid the cash in the plainly marked box under my bathroom sink. Not one coin was ever stolen.

NOT EXACTLY THE US POST OFFICE

We lived on Santa Rosa Street in the gated Magallanes Village, in Makati Rizal, Philippines. Incoming mail was delivered to the Embassy. Outgoing mail was sent through the Embassy or the military APO (Army Post Office) at Seafront.

USAID wives took turns driving or going by taxi to the Embassy every day. Your maid would deliver other family's mail on-foot to the different households. We did something similar when sending mail to our husbands in Vietnam. Mail through regular channels could take weeks.

We knew when a husband was going to arrive in Manila to visit his family. There was an unwritten rule. Never call on a family when the husband was visiting from Saigon unless you were invited. A husband's visit was treasured, private family time. When we knew one of the men was in-country, we would have our maid hand-deliver our letters to his house. He would hand-carry the letters to Saigon. When your husband was home, there was a constant ding-dong of the door bell, but everyone was glad to take their turn.

PROTOCOL AND ETIQUETTE

Embassy protocol is polite and formal tradition. It is also a reminder that you represent the people of the United States while in the Foreign Service. The calling card is a diplomatic necessity. Within a few days of arrival at a new Post, protocol required my husband to make an Official visit, first to the Chief of Mission and then to the Ambassador. A small silver dish was always near the front door for the mandatory calling card. It was three and a half by two inches, white, with the entire formal name of Albert Hayden Stone Jr. printed in the exact middle. Once he made his Calls, I made mine. I was required to call on the wives of these two diplomats leaving two of my husband's cards: one for the wife and one for her husband.

Ambassador Blair was no longer at Post so the Philippines had no Ambassador when I arrived as a "Saigon wife." Only a visit to the wife of the Chief of Mission was required. The Saigon Mission families did not belong to the Philippine Mission so we were not included in any Official functions and felt at times like the poor relative that was never invited to the party.

When G. Mennen "Soapy" Williams, the former governor of Michigan and heir to the Mennen fortune, was assigned as our new Ambassador, he and his wife greeted the Embassy and military personnel at Post with an informal Open House at the Residence. An invitation list was sent out with a scheduled time for each group. Buses were sent to pick us up at our appointed time. We were on the very bottom of that list as "Saigon Wives and Stragglers."

I was nervous about my first meeting with an Ambassador and his wife, but felt more comfortable when the Ambassador greeted me in his trademark green bow tie with white polka dots, and his very charming and informal wife met me at the door dressed in tights as an elf—or maybe it was a pixie. I don't remember which holiday the date was near, but have the feeling it was Christmas.

The Mission always made sure that each family had a sponsor upon arrival. Women at the Post were expected to volunteer. Most were glad to do it.

If the Mission did not provide housing, your sponsor would help with the house hunting. If the Post provided your housing, she would meet you at your new house the day you arrived and see to it that you had a minimum supply of groceries in the refrigerator. She would hire (usually two) maids which you were not obligated to keep. It was her duty to explain Embassy services, help register the kids in school, show you the best places to shop, and if necessary, act as translator. I sponsored quite a few women and found it fun. One of the newcomers I felt obligated to sponsor. She had my name—Nancy Stone. We became good friends. She was tiny so she became little Nancy. Unfortunately, at five foot six, I became big Nancy.

Your sponsor was your escort on the Call to the wife of the Chief of Mission, your husband's boss. The wife of the Chief of Mission took you to visit the wife of the Ambassador.

On the days the wives of these two diplomats were receiving, typically four or five newcomers and their escorts would visit for thirty to forty-five minutes. You were expected to wear a dress and gloves. Many wore hats, as well. Tea and coffee and some sort of sweet were served.

At that time, I had very few opinions about anything that was important to these women. Many were world travelers. They knew people who made very important decisions. I had been busy raising kids and taking college courses at night and hadn't paid much attention to what was going in the world. I felt very awkward and out of place.

> **Lessons learned:** When you lift your cup, teaspoons and cookies slide to the center of your saucer so you can't put your cup down. Brownies leave yucky stuff between your teeth. You will be asked a question as soon as you take a bite. Never eat with your gloves on. Buy a book on etiquette.

THE AMERICAN SCHOOL

The Embassy gave me a check in American currency to pay the school tuition. A neighbor whose husband worked for GAO (Government Accounting Office) said she would show me the best way to pay the fees. She took me to a nearby house where a man converted the dollars into enough pesos to pay the tuition with lots of pesos left over. I wrote Al that I had found this great way to get additional money. Instead of being happy, he was furious. Turns out they call that the Black Market and I could be sent back to the States for using it. Or worse, Al could lose his job. I had a lot to learn.

The American School was difficult, competitive, and highly diversified. Most of the student body consisted of children of diplomatic families from the various embassies in-country. Often the sons or daughters of the president of the country would attend. It exposed our children to cultures from all over the world. The student's nearly total absence of racial bias was wonderful to witness. Adults could take some lessons from them.

We found the schools excellent. All of the American schools in our experience were academically oriented. There were no classes that were not "reading', writing', or arithmetic." Everyone attended a full day of academic classes. The end result was a good education.

It was hotter than blazes with no air-conditioning, so the school day began and ended early. The school bus arrived at six-thirty a.m. Weather affected the classes in other ways too. The roofs in all the countries tended to be corrugated metal, no matter how fancy the structure. That meant little or no insulation from the heat and a lot of noise from the rain. There were times during monsoon season when the school had to close because no one could hear anything being said over the noisy rain beating on the roof.

Another problem was the library—or lack thereof. Homework research became a difficult task with no good source for research material. Some of the families had purchased an Encyclopedia Britannica or something similar. We had a huge collection of National Geographic magazines and had many requests to borrow them. All of the families shared. We sure could have used the computers of today.

GROCERY SHOPPING 101-103

We ate most meals at home. That meant lots of trips to the local markets to buy food that might—or might not—be safe to eat. "Night soil" was often used for fertilizer. Human excrement might be great on plants, but I sure didn't want it on my plate. Most houses had a second "dirty" kitchen sink that was used to wash and soak fruits and vegetables. Leafy vegetables were hard to clean. Nasty little bugs and slimy dirt had to be coaxed out of hiding places. The quickest and easiest way to clean was to drop everything in a bath of diluted bleach. I found myself becoming philosophical about the process. If anything escaped the scrubbing, at least it was dead.

In Manila, there were open air markets selling Lechon (a national dish that is a whole, stuffed, barbecued pig), a jillion kinds of rice, wonderful mangoes, calamancie (a cross between a lime and a lemon for their version of lemonade), pineapples, and plantain.

Our district, called Makati, looked out of place. It was a small area of a few square blocks of modern high rises. It did offer a large, modern "Super." Products on the shelves had unfamiliar names. The rice was in huge baskets on the floor, but the market looked much like those in the States. One huge difference was the armed guards in uniform at the end of the aisles where you would ordinarily expect to see a display of canned soup. Their main purpose was to watch for shop lifters. They were often untrained and overly aggressive.

Tropical fruits were plentiful and delicious, but not the vegetables. I didn't think I would ever get emotional about a perfectly round tomato, but I remember welling up with tears when seeing one back in a State-side produce market. Sorely missing was fruit like peaches, pears, grapes, and apples.

The meat department looked fairly normal except for the live shrimp which always seemed to get loose in the trunk of the taxi. We had to buy extra eggs because they were displayed loose in a box and carried in a paper sack. Good luck getting them home in one piece.

At times the milk was tubercular. The Embassy would notify us when the milk was bad. Bugs were often in packaged goods. We stored as much as we could of the goods like flour and sugar in the refrigerator or freezer. Many things, like crackers and cookies, were sold in metal cans. Roaches were a problem in every country.

Poultry does not do well in the tropics. Chickens were tiny, almost Cornish hen size. Turkeys, if you could find one, were the size of a large chicken. Beef was tough. Pork was actually darned good. The national dish is a tasty chicken and pork dish called Adobo served with the always present rice. Patis is a foul smelling fish sauce.

The small commissary at Seafront was available to us. We could buy cigarettes, liquor with no taxes, canned or packaged food staples, and items like shaving cream and band-aids. Holiday candies would come in at times. There was a tiny APO for mailing packages and buying stamps, a pool, tennis court, and a tiny restaurant. Seafront became our home away from home. We "lived" at the pool.

The commissaries at Clark Air Force Base and Sangley Naval Base were also available. Neither was convenient. It was hours to Clark over a road sometimes terrorized by Huks, Philippine guerillas. Sangley was a little over an hour by car. The road was bumpy and dusty, but not dangerous unless you count dodging the caribou.

The fastest way to Sangley was by the launch that went back and forth over the bay from the Embassy. We took it on occasion, but the bay is wide with huge waves that can quickly make you wish you were on firm ground. I remember the loud crack of the waves hitting the small boat. We would stop dead in the water for a scary second. To make matters worse, if one person threw up, everyone else turned green. Besides, you could only buy what you could carry if you took the launch. In the car, we took ice chests and loaded up.

JUST LIKE A DATE

Al was able to travel to the Philippines for three and half days every six weeks. He would arrive early afternoon on Thursday and leave early Monday morning. The first few times he came in, we would meet him at the airport and go directly home. The kids and I would compete for his attention all weekend long. I'm sure the kids were just as frustrated as I was before the weekend was over. It was hard on Al too. We had to find a way to fix the problem.

I went to several hotels in Manila and told them I wanted an early check-in at no extra charge and that I would be doing it regularly for the next eighteen months. The Sheraton agreed. When it was time, I went to the hotel on Thursday morning and arranged for dinner on the balcony. The room was set up with wine, a fondue pot, cheese and crackers, and the slinkiest nightgown I could find. I took Al from the airport to the hotel, instead of home. The kids knew they wouldn't see him until the next morning, but that he was all theirs from then on.

It was a great idea. We had a date-to-remember every six weeks. Al loved it, the hotel loved it, and the kids were happy. I have to admit that I sometimes wondered what other hotel guests thought when I was so well known at the hotel. I was obviously a "regular," but it wasn't clear what kind. When other women with husbands in Vietnam heard about our plan, the Sheraton and other hotels were soon doing a land-office business with the "Saigon wives."

These special weekends became something to look forward to. They were like dating all over again—with no restrictions. It was also fun to sit back and watch Al with the kids. We all planned and came up with fun and interesting things to do and places to go. This is a stark contrast to most families in the States who come home from work exhausted every night, cook dinner, help with homework, and go to bed. We had a cook and staff to help with everything and built-in baby-sitters.

Even though the kids and I had to manage without Al most of the time during the assignment in the Philippines, we have wonderful memories of these great times.

LANGUAGE AND CULTURE

There are more than one-hundred and twenty languages spoken in the Republic of the Philippines. Spanish was the original language of the country. English was added as a second official language in 1935. Because there are so many languages, Tagalog, later renamed *Filipino*, was chosen as the base regional language. Following the American occupation, English became the official language. That is a lot of fuss over language. I am just happy that I didn't have to learn a new language in addition to everything else at my first Post overseas.

I hired a woman to come to the house and teach us Tagalog. We didn't do very well. For one thing we found very few Filipinos that would let us practice the language with them. Guess they wanted to show off their English instead. I still remember a few phrases. Mabuhay is the Filipino "Aloha," meaning "hello" and "good-bye." Salamat po is "Thank you very much." Kamusta kayo is "How are you." And Maligayang Pasko is "Merry Christmas." (Limited usage!) The national anthem was sung in every movie theater. The kids knew every word.

In the home, Al and I were called "Ma'am" and "Sir" as in, "Is Sir coming home this weekend?" We had a cook (English word), an amah (Asian word) to watch the younger children and a lavendera (Spanish word) to do the wash. Most Filipinos liked Americans—and idolized General MacArthur. He and the United States brought them freedom, mandatory public education, and financial assistance.

It took months for our freight, which included the washer and dryer, to catch up with us each time we moved. Until we could get a clothesline up, our clothes were washed by hand and spread over bushes to dry, as they do in the provinces. Articles of clothing were disappearing from our back yard. We couldn't imagine how they were getting out of a seven-foot walled yard. Then someone saw the neighbor's pet monkey helping himself to some underwear. I had to go four or five houses down and knock on the door to retrieve our clothes.

Imelda Marcos was a beautiful woman. She was a beauty queen in the Miss Universe contest. Almost every taxi had a picture of her. I swear everyone in the country watches the Miss Universe contest every year. President Nixon came to visit the Philippines while we were there. Buildings were spruced up, flowers were planted, and curbs were painted along his route. Miss Philippines didn't win the contest that year, but the turnout to welcome her was twice the turnout for the President.

You often saw the men taxi drivers with at least one, very long fingernail on the little finger. By long, I mean inches, and they curled and twisted, hanging down and brown in color. Not sure why taxi drivers, in particular. Maybe that was just my exposure to this practice.

Many years ago it was a sign of wealth to have long, useless fingernails. The very wealthy wore all their nails grossly long to signify that they did not have to work. The binding of women's feet in China comes from the same idea. They had to be carried everywhere—and certainly were not expected to work.

The main mode of transportation was a uniquely Filipino vehicle called a jeepney. Many jeeps were left behind after the war. The Filipinos added a covered extension on the back for eight passengers, painted flowers and bright designs all over them and charged a fee for a ride. They were inexpensive, readily available, and fun to ride in.

MY FRIEND, THE COLONEL

On the way to the Philippines from San Francisco, we made two stops. The first was in Hawaii. I herded everyone off the plane only to find that it was nearly time to herd them back on again.

When we landed in Guam, I decided it was too much trouble for the few minutes we would be in the airport and stayed on the plane. Aside from being too darned hot, it worked out fine. The kids ran up and down the aisle and stretched more than they would have inside the airport.

A Filipino man stayed behind with me. I was rather suspicious at first, but somehow he seemed "okay" and we talked a little. He was a Colonel in the Philippine Army and had been the bodyguard to President Garcia's wife, the First Lady of the Philippines (prior to Imelda Marcos). After landing in the Philippines, I never dreamed I would ever see the Colonel again.

We hadn't been in Manila very long, when there was a knock on the door. It was the Colonel's driver. The Colonel had come to visit in a military jeep with the driver and another soldier. I invited him in, but he wanted to talk outside.

As the kids and I chatted with him, Janice kept eyeing the jeep. He asked her if she wanted to go for a ride around the block. I had all the other kids with me and there was little room in the jeep so, like a fool, I let her get in. They drove away—and didn't come back. I have only felt panic like that a few times in my life. It is an indescribable feeling when you know you have done something terribly stupid and may have put a child in danger.

Thank Heaven the Colonel had given me his home address earlier. I had no car, so Butch and I ran to find a taxi to take us to the Colonel's house. Even the ride to his house was scary, as I had no idea where in the world I was. The jeep was parked in front. We knocked on the door and his wife let us in. Janice was there, well provided for with cookies, cake, and all sorts of goodies at the kitchen table having a wonderful time. He seemed surprised that I was so concerned and apologized, but I had a real scare.

I was grateful to have him as a friend. We had been in Manila only a few weeks when twelve-year-old Butch asked to go to an evening teen-age function at the Embassy. Several of his friends were going and one of the fathers had volunteered to drive. Three hours later, the kids were picked up, but Butch wasn't with them. There was no police department to call, but we had the Colonel. I used the neighbor's phone and called him. It was now 11:00 o'clock at night. He sent a jeep and several men to help us. We enlisted a few more neighbors. They drove back and forth between our house and the Embassy. Car after car returned to the house with nothing. There was an open-air market on the way to the Embassy that I had never had to nerve to venture into. If Butch was walking, he had to pass right by it. All I could think of was a kidnapping or an attack.

During all the commotion, Butch ambled into the house. He had gone to the restroom and his friends left without him. He couldn't call me so he decided to walk. He was fine, but had received his first offer from a prostitute that night at the market. I got a lesson in raising a teen-ager in a third-world country.

The Colonel remained my friend during the eighteen months I stayed in-country. He and his wife came to dinner several times when Al was home. As was the tradition, they always brought a wonderful gift of a carving or one of the many beautiful hand-made crafts found in the Philippines. When an American was invited to a Filipino home, the gift to the host was usually liquor, cigarettes, or candy. We could buy these items at the Commissary at a fraction of the cost Nationals paid on the local market. Not quite so nice a gift as a carving, but always appreciated.

The Colonel had a small upright piano that his son had played when he was living at home. The heat, humidity, and a few bugs had played havoc with the hammers and felt pads. I offered to have it repaired if I could use it while living in Manila. He agreed. I loved having the piano and it was returned to him in excellent condition. A good deal for both of us.

Just before I moved away, his son married. We were invited to the wedding. Al couldn't be in-country on that date. I accepted and took Butch as my escort as it was not considered good etiquette for a woman to attend a function alone.

The weddings there are often at an early hour. After an 8:00 a.m. wedding and mass, we moved to a very large hall that was beautifully decorated. Many tables were set for breakfast. As people were being seated, they released a huge, hanging basket of white doves. The Colonel made it a point to introduce Butch and me to his guests as his "American friends." I hadn't realized how proud he was of that.

And then the worst ...

I was wearing a hand-embroidered dress made of piña, a cloth woven from pineapple fiber. Piña is considered very formal. In lieu of black-tie and tails, which would be far too warm in that weather, the men wear beautifully embroidered shirts of piña called barong-tagalog which are lightweight and worn untucked. The fabric is an ecru color and shows stains very prominently, it turned out.

The Colonel seated Butch and me. There was a fruit compote already on the table in a stemmed dish. The compote served there is always sort of a soupy consistency, probably because of the heat. Somehow I managed to put one of my breasts precisely in the fruit compote dish, knocking it over into my lap. Several waiters appeared and tried to remove the sticky fruit and goop. Because of the location of the goop, it was more than a little awkward. They handed me towels to try to dry the dress. I now had a big wet spot over my chest and another in the middle of my lap. I looked like a little kid who couldn't wait! To make matters worse, when the spots finally dried, they got stiff and remained just as well marked and obvious as they did when they were wet. I'm not sure how proud the Colonel was then of his American friend.

Thank Heaven I had my driver, Macario, that day. After eating at the hall, Macario drove us home. I changed clothes and went to the Colonel's house to watch the bride and groom open their gifts. I am afraid what I chose was also a big disappointment. (We may have looked wealthy to the Filipinos, but we were still trying to recover from Al's college days in those first couple of years overseas and weren't exactly rolling in money.) I think the Colonel wanted to show off his American friend's gift. I wished I had thought of that before buying the set of bowls.

Even with the wedding disaster, we still saw quite a bit of the Colonel's family after the wedding. He and his wife are probably still saying, "Remember that crazy American lady?"

IT WASN'T THE FLU

I have such guilt feelings about this whole experience. I have tried and tried to think what I could have done differently—but it really doesn't matter because what happened is in the past and can't be changed.

With five children, illnesses that come along usually "hit" one or two, then are passed on to one or two more. Hopefully, it doesn't make a second cycle by re-infecting those who already suffered through it. The kids and I took turns being miserable with the flu for nearly two weeks. One by one, we began to feel better. Seven-year old Kenny didn't improve.

The Embassy doctor was available two days a week. Kenny and I were waiting at his door on his next appointment day. He ran some tests which didn't help at all. Kenny kept vomiting and vomiting and suffered constant, foul-smelling diarrhea. He kept losing weight. The Embassy advised us to go either to a local hospital or to the large military hospital at Clark Air Force Base which was ninety-five kilometers to the north. The local hospital was not an option.

Ordinarily, the Embassy would have provided a car and driver. This time they not only refused to give me transportation to Clark, but wouldn't grant me permission to drive my own car.

The country was under martial law due to the activity of the Huks (Hukbalahap guerrillas). The road to Clark, in addition to being poorly paved and crowded with foot traffic and caribou, was right through the middle of an area where the Huks were attacking cars on the road. They were taking people hostage or even killing them. It wasn't safe.

I had made friends with Carole, another Saigon wife. Her husband, Jim "Maggie" Megellas, was head of CORDS (Civil Operations and Revolutionary Development Support). He had an equivalent rank of Major General.

> **For the record:** Jim is the most decorated soldier of the 82nd airborne battalion to this day and was recently nominated for the Medal of Honor.

Carole could reach her husband in northern Vietnam through a one-way MARS (Military Auxiliary Radio System) radio. We had no authorization, but finally reached Al through Jim's office. Al immediately requested permission to come home. He was denied.

We couldn't wait. Kenny had lost almost a third of his body weight.

We owe Jim a lot. He arranged for a plane. Al flew into the Philippines the next morning without permission and—since the Embassy held his papers—no passport. When he arrived at the house, we piled everyone into our car, said more than a few prayers, and left for Clark.

Deciding what to do about the other four kids had been difficult. The Huks seemed relatively quiet and they were the main worry. School was in session and they were safer at home, but there were only two women we felt comfortable to ask for help. They were both visiting their husbands in Vietnam. We had no idea what we would encounter at the hospital or how long we might have to stay. All of us went together for the six-hour, sixty mile ride. People and livestock crowded the road. It took forever to get through the villages. We inched our way.

Clark, at that time, was the largest Air Force Base in the world. It was literally a city with theaters, schools, movie theaters, shopping, and restaurants—and a wonderful hospital. Kenny was given several tests right away. They found the problem. He had contracted Tropical Sprue. His body was not producing folic acid so he was unable to digest food properly. Undigested food left his body any way it could. He was starving to death.

The doctors allowed us to keep Kenny with us overnight. With Al's rank, we were able to take advantage of the very elegant Officer's Mess and had nice quarters in a motel on base. We took a vote and decided to see John Wayne in *True Grit* at the theater. Kenny and I didn't see much of the movie. I took him to the bathroom again and again. He would have been more comfortable back in the room, but he wanted to stay. I didn't argue.

The next day we were told that the doctors wanted to keep Kenny for a few days to make sure he responded to the medication. The treatment was really simple. All we had to do was give him folic acid in pill form—and watch him like a hawk.

Now we had to decide what to do. We stayed with Kenny all that day. He wasn't hospitalized yet, so we took the kids on a tour of the fire station. The firemen let the kids play in the fire truck. There happened to be a talent show that day, so we all went.

Kenny was admitted the next morning. The nurses were fantastic and Kenny seemed to love them all. We had to decide whether to stay for several more days, keeping the kids out of school or to leave Kenny and come back for him. The poor little guy didn't act sick. He just looked thin and pale. The doctors had stopped the vomiting and diarrhea. Visiting his room was awkward because either Al or I had to stay in the lobby with the other children.

The most crucial factor was that Al was in-country illegally and in danger of losing his job for leaving Vietnam without permission. He had to leave. I don't know if I just felt so comfortable with the hospital staff, or that they kept saying it would be "fine," but the decision was made to leave Kenny, get the other kids back in school, and find someone to stay with them so I could get back to the hospital. Right or wrong—we left. I still do not know if that was the right decision. I do know it was one of the hardest I ever made. We took a photo of him as we were leaving. The expression on his face still haunts me.

Al drove us home, said good-by, and left. A Saigon wife was due back from Vietnam the next day. She agreed to stay at our house with her daughter.

> **Note:** Kenny's teacher appeared at the door with get well letters written by all of his classmates. As far as I know, Ken still has them. They were wonderful.

I tried to call Kenny at the hospital from the neighbor's house. There are so many illegal phone hook-ups that legitimate phones can't get service. It took a frustrating twenty minutes just to get a dial tone. I finally got through and was able to tell Kenny I was on my way. I found out later he was just fine until I called. Then he started to cry. Big mistake. I felt terrible.

The nurses said they were only going to watch him, but Ken told me later that they did some testing and it wasn't very pleasant. That made me feel even worse. Thank God the Embassy decided I could return to Clark. They provided me with a car and an armed driver. We went that day.

Kenny dealt with the disease until we arrived permanently back in the States. Sprue is endemic to tropical areas. People who live in these areas tend not to get it. People conditioned to changing seasons that move to the tropics, do. The hope was that when he got back to the States, it would go away. It did. We know we caused this to happen to our son. That is a harsh reality to live with.

BLACK MAGIC EXISTS

Black magic or voodoo has many names. It can be called upon for good or evil. We encountered wok-wok in the Philippines.

When we realized liquor was disappearing from our liquor cabinet, I questioned our new cook and the maids. When I talked to the maids, tears welled up and they clutched each other. The cook was calm and simply denied any knowledge. Hmmm.

I thought the two maids might feel more comfortable with someone who spoke Tagalog, their native language, so I asked for help from a USAID wife who was a Filipina. We decided to question the two maids on the cook's night off. It worked. Both maids began to sob and said the cook was stealing the liquor. She had threatened them with wok-wok if they dared to say anything.

It took a lot of prompting, but they finally took us into their bedroom and opened the bottom dresser drawer. Two neatly stacked piles of underclothing of each of the women were in the middle of the otherwise empty drawer. Resting across the two stacks was the magic charm; a vanilla extract bottle filled with what looked like seaweed and shells. They were absolutely convinced that the wok-wok would make boils erupt all over their bodies.

As my friend leaned over to pick up the bottle, both maids gasped aloud, fell against the wall, and slid down to the floor. When they opened their eyes, she was holding the bottle. They visibly shook as they looked again and again at their arms and legs. They seemed dumbfounded when nothing appeared on their skin. Tears of relief began to trickle.

Their ordeal did nothing to convince them there was no power in that charm. They decided the "magic" had transferred to my friend.

I fired the cook.

OVER THE RAPIDS WITH GRANDMA

My Mother came to visit us for Christmas. We were looking for something new and different to do. Al was home for the holiday, so we would do it together.

I kept hearing about Pagsanjan Falls. They could be reached only by boat over white water. We heard it was beautiful, and it was fairly close by. Why I thought going there was such a great idea with little kids and a grandmother, I have no idea. It turned out to be lots of fun and one of those things you should try once in your life. We certainly would not have gone though if I had known beforehand how many people had been hurt in that white water.

> **Note:** It is scary now to think about some of the things we did and probably should not have. Thankfully, we got through it all okay. This will sound corny, but whenever I did something with Al, I felt safe. He was an ex-Marine, had good instincts, survival skills, fierce loyalties, and was physically strong. I always felt that he would never let anything happen to us. That

was probably asking too much, but it led to a lot of adventure we never would have attempted otherwise.

We met our guides on the river. Only two of us were allowed in each boat as there was a guide in front and a guide in back of each pair. Butch and Jim went together. I had Janice. My Mother had Kenny, and Al had Eric.

Incidentally, boat means a banca which is carved from logs in the shape of a canoe. You sit low in the bottom. Each of our guides had a long pole that was used to keep us away from boulders and other hazards in the narrow river. The real danger was many very sharp, almost right hand turns, in the river itself. If the turns were not enough to worry about, many of them had huge, six to eight foot tall, and four to five foot wide, boulders sitting dead in the middle. It was easy to see how people got hurt—or died, depending on the force of the water.

The scenery on the way to the white water was serene and beautiful. The narrow river wound through a three-canopy jungle that hugged the water's edge. One side of the river was a steep, rocky cliff with waterfalls falling gracefully over orchids and wonderful vines. You could hear birds calling in the jungle. We saw a few monkeys.

Eventually, we pulled up to a flat place on the bank. We were guided up a narrow path with the jungle poking us on either side. The path opened onto a clearing that held a little cluster of nipa (palm) huts. Chickens clucked here and there and two curious piglets came to greet us. In the very center was a large platform with open walls made of bamboo. That was our restaurant. They served rice and chicken with fruit and coconut. It was simple and good.

We were the highlight of the day. A crowd gathered around the outside of the building and watched us eat. They smiled at us and we smiled back. After lunch we said our good-byes and climbed back into the bancas.

Then the excitement began.

Everything was perfect. The water was moving fast enough to be exciting and a few of the turns were pretty wild, but the men were very skillful and kept us moving safely. It was frightening to careen down the river, heading straight for an enormous boulder, only to turn suddenly away. The men were hopping in and out of the bancas first on one side, then on the other. They pushed their poles here and there, keeping all the bancas together, and out of harm's way.

I remember wishing I had asked more questions about where the river met the falls. I wondered if there was any danger that we might go over the darned thing. As the water settled down, we realized that we were hearing the beginnings of what later became a deafening roar. The bancas slipped into a water-filled gorge with high, rocky cliffs on four sides. High above us water from an unseen river was being funneled into a very small opening in the cliff. It was coming straight out like a freight train on our side of the gorge. It spewed way out and then dropped into the gorge with a huge water rainbow. It was so thunderous you literally could not hear conversation. With less water, it would not be as spectacular, but it was incredible on that day. It was a great day, but sure wouldn't advise it after a monsoon rain.

BAGUIO GUEST HOUSE

Baguio, the City of the Pines, is a mountain town in the northern Philippines at an elevation of four thousand, five hundred feet. It is the center of the gold-mining region. The web site today reads, "A beautiful resort in the mountains, it features a Jack Niclaus designed golf course as well as hotels, a shopping center and a convention center." John Hay was a military and Department of Defense R&R (rest and recreation) center in our day. I don't recall even one nice hotel in town.

When my Mother came to visit, we took a trip to Baguio. There is an airport now, but we had to drive there. It is about seven hours from Manila. It's not far, but caribou and foot traffic on poor roads slowed us down. As we began the climb into the mountains, the road became narrow and winding. We passed villages of thatched huts nestled in the crevices of the young, sharp, green mountains.

We had reserved the five-bedroom Embassy guest house on Camp John Hay. Poor planning on someone's part placed the entrance road right through the middle of the holes of the golf course. Flying golf balls were a challenge each time we went in or out of the Camp. The house itself was large and beautiful. Two maids were provided. The only heat was an enormous fireplace in the dining room. Baguio gets very cool at night, so we froze in the bedrooms.

Al took the kids horseback riding. The house had a ping-pong table and games. The central market was the main attraction. The Filipinos decorate so many things with exquisite hand-embroidery work. They make beautiful bowls, figures, and everything imaginable from capiz, a translucent sea shell, and wonderfully grained woods. We visited a silver "factory." People were sitting on long benches hand-making filigree jewelry of silver. The delicate and beautiful pieces looked like they were made of lace.

The kid's memories vary a little from mine.

> **Janice recalls:** I remember Dad taking us to a silver factory and my experience with the beggar woman in the market place. There was an old lady all dressed in black with a hunched back.

> She had a little handkerchief with a few coins in it. When she came up to me, she scared the living daylights out of me. I clawed my way up Dad's back. She must have thought I was nuts. I climbed Dad's back like it was a tree! I also remember seeing a little boy dragging himself in the dirt because he had no legs. This freaked me out as well. Not too fond of the market I guess.

Begging is a reality in any third-world country. Many of the unfortunate are maimed or crippled. Some are even known to main themselves or their own children to gain sympathy. It is a sad condition and difficult to witness.

NOTHING LIKE THE BROCHURE

We kept hearing about Hundred Islands in a remote area in northern Luzon, and decided to go for a weekend trip. The brochure made it sound wonderful. We were going to stay in a nipa hut on stilts at the beach. We drove and drove—and drove—over a windy, narrow road with chunks of cement and slow-moving caribou. There were seven of us in the car with no air-conditioning, so the trip took considerable stamina.

The kids say they remember Hundred Islands as the most beautiful beach of all. The little islands were very small, some ten to fifteen feet across, some up to one hundred-feet high. They were eroded around the bottom so you couldn't get near enough to climb them. The water had varied depths, but you could be a long way from shore and still stand up.

The sand was fine and pure white. The water was warm, with colorful fish swimming around. The coral was young with beautiful reds, blues, and bright whites. Live coral, versus the mostly dead and gray coral in Hawaii, is amazing.

That is where the resemblance to the brochure ended. Our hut was on stilts and hidden in waves that washed back and forth. A skimpy ladder ran up to the open entry. There was nothing inside except seven cots—unless you want to include all the multi-legged critters hiding in the nipa. The "bathroom" was a three-sided pile of corrugated metal sheets which were propped up on poles on the beach. It was not tall enough to stand up in. It included a huge snorting pig that hovered near the "door." The "cooking facility" was a circle of rocks on the beach. Thank goodness I had brought a few pots and the liquid heating sterno that I always took everywhere—just in case.

We thought there was a kitchen, so I had loaded up things like Rice-a-Roni and food that needed to be cooked. The first night we bought some rice and meat from a Sari Sari stand on the beach that sold mostly soda pop and snack food. Heaven only knows what we actually ate that night.

The next day, we piled up the rocks and put the sterno can in the middle. That was our stove. With no other store for miles, we ate mostly eggs and whatever we had in a can, and filled up on the Sari Sari rice. It actually wasn't too bad, but you could cook only one thing at a time.

Sleeping in the hut seemed like fun at first. Do you have any idea how loud waves are, especially at high tide? They kept everyone awake and, in the dark, we were all wondering where the bugs were. There was no electricity, so we decided to leave one candle burning. With no glass in the windows, I kept hoping the blowing wind wouldn't knock it over and set the hut on fire.

Al decided to go down the ladder for something or other and got his Levis soaked. I will never forget how those jeans smelled as they dried. The rank odor of dying fish would have been an improvement.

Miraculously, no one got a tummy ache. It was truly a peaceful and beautiful weekend—except for that darned pig.

MEMORIES ON THE BATAAN PENINSULA AND CORREGIDOR ISLAND

One of the most important historical sites in the Philippines is the island of Corregidor. This was the last stronghold of General MacArthur. US and Filipino soldiers on that island were included in the nearly seventy-thousand that surrendered to the Japanese in 1942. They were transferred to the Bataan Peninsula and forced to march about sixty miles to a prison camp in the north. The prisoners were beaten, shot, beheaded, and bayoneted. They suffered from malaria, dehydration, and dysentery. Asking for water or falling behind meant death. The rare handful of food was contaminated rice. An estimated seven to ten thousand died.

Corregidor is an island near the Bataan Peninsula in the entrance to the huge Manila Bay. When we traveled to the island, it looked pretty much as it did when the Army left. I bought tickets on the one ferry that would take you there. A jeepney picked us up at our home and took us to the beautiful Manila Hotel on the bay. We boarded the ferry at the hotel pier. It took several hours to travel the thirty miles to the tip of the Bataan Peninsula.

The boat dropped anchor off a white sand beach. I was wishing I hadn't worn a skirt. We had to climb over the side of the ferry onto a rope ladder and down into bancas. We were served lunch on the beach. Jim decided to investigate an old, weathered, hulk of a wooden boat on the beach and rammed some of the rotting wood up under his fingernails. I still get chills when I think of it. There was a nurse with the group, but the first aid kit was on board the ferry. She took Jim back to the ship and removed the splinters. His fingers were sore for a very long time.

We returned to the ferry and that darned rope ladder, and made the short trip to Corregidor. The beach itself was not composed of sand, but small, smooth stones. Many of the stones had a reddish-brown swirl in them. The story is that the swirl is the blood from the many that died there. I don't know if it is true or not, but it certainly drove home the horror that beach must have been.

There were wooden buildings around. Many were in disrepair. There were some abandoned vehicles. Most of the men and women had lived in the huge Malinta Tunnel, an amazing labyrinth of tunnels that housed a hospital, living quarters, weapons, and equipment.

Guess we would be impressed with the island tour today. You can spend the night. How wonderful that a place of such struggle, death, and sadness could evolve into a place of peace and restfulness. The tour goes through the tunnel. The side tunnels are illuminated so that you can see how they used the space for the wounded, sleeping and storage. We need to visit these battlegrounds and remember that we are free today because our men and women died there.

I was sorry that my Mother didn't get to the island. It was high on her list of things to see. She and Janice had reservations and then got as far as the hotel, but something happened to the ferry. She had to return to the States before the ferry was repaired.

Our Makati House

Jeepney

Caribou

Pagsanjan Falls

SAIGON, VIETNAM

February 1968 to February 1970

Al helped the Vietnamese people during a terrible war. I had to live in the Philippines with the children while he lived and worked in Saigon, but I did visit him several times.

THE VIETNAMESE EXPERIENCE

Except for the pilots and one other man, Al's plane from Hong Kong to Saigon was empty. They landed at Tan Son Nut airport the day after the big Tet attack. The airport was empty. Most of its roof was missing. No one from the Embassy was there to meet him. Someone with a jeep offered to drive him into town to find a military BOQ (Bachelor Officers' Quarters) to spend the night. They were all full, but he finally located a hotel. He ran next door to grab a bite and tried to sneak back to the hotel just minutes after the six o'clock curfew. The door was locked. The shooting started. He spent a good part of the evening behind a cement garden planter before he could crawl to safety. Welcome to Saigon.

As a Program Officer under the direction of Bill Colby (who later became Director of the CIA), Al settled into an office in an outer building within the Embassy walls. He was assigned the job of writing the budget and logistically supporting thirty-three private and government agencies (such as Catholic Relief, World Vision, OXFAM, CARE, and Doctors Without Borders) into the Refugee Program. He was awarded the medal for Civilian Service in Vietnam, a plaque for service to the Refugee Program and nominated for an award from the Vietnamese government which he was not allowed to accept.

The Viet Cong leveled and burned village after village. This forced the residents to find shelter in Refugee Camps over what became known as the *Street Without Joy*. There were reports of tortured and mutilated leaders and villagers. Reports of rockets going off on both sides of the road creating huge bubbles in the rice paddies. Other reports told of bodies floating down rivers.

Al made frequent trips to the provinces to inspect the camps and sadly, to the villages to report the number of dead men, women, and children. These were not casual trips. Most were by Air America, a US civilian airline that was covertly operated by the CIA during the War. According to Al, most of these harrowing flights were in small, ancient planes piloted by dare-devils. They flew low over the jungle to avoid being shot down. They landed and took-off under impossible circumstances. They flew in, around, and over the war.

Al tells a story of a Congressman who accompanied him and a co-worker on an inspection tour. They were in the village only minutes when they were attacked. Terrified, the Congressman ran back to the plane and ordered the pilot to leave—without Al and his co-worker. The two men weren't picked up until the next day after a miserable nightmare night dodging bullets in a soggy rice paddy.

There was a lot of good with the bad. There are too many events to relate them all. I have good memories of one man in particular who was an employee of World Vision. I met Gene in Al's office. He was snitching pencils off the desk for "his boys." Al found money to fund his project and the two of them began the "Street Boys Project." As far as I know, this venture was the only project that the Vietnamese government continued when the Americans left.

Gene spoke almost no Vietnamese, but that didn't stop him from setting up a shelter in a deserted police station for as many as thirty boys. They ranged in age from about nine to early teens. He prowled the alleys and hung around the jail looking for orphan boys. They were offered a place to sleep, food donated from restaurants twice a day, and minimal medical care. Some boys were too frightened. Some were too sick. The group decided who could stay and who should go. Once accepted, if someone stole or caused trouble, a vote was taken. He was either punished or thrown back on the streets.

I enjoyed gathering things like T-shirts, books, flip-flop sandals, and candy to take to them on each of my trips. I borrowed a film from my Embassy on one occasion. The only thing available was a travelogue about Las Vegas. Bob, Al's roommate, spoke fluent Vietnamese and volunteered to translate. The boys loved it. We played it over and over. They were fascinated by all the lights and the bustle.

> **Lesson learned:** I was warned not to be too friendly on a personal level with these boys. I was told that Asian men and boys rejected touching and direct eye contact by female outsiders. What I found was that the boys responded to genuine affection and hugs when they were scared and lonely in a war zone without parents or family.

Al taught a night class in English in a corner schoolroom on the second floor. During one of their breaks, a female student planted a bomb. It blew out the two outside walls. Thank God no one was in the room at the time. The popular class lost its appeal.

Al worked with some interesting and wonderful people. Bob Wolff was a Lutheran Minister married to a Thai woman. Bob was best known for going out into the middle of a three-canopy jungle in Thailand and building a Leper colony. He wrote an excellent book about his adventure called "Village of the

Outcasts." The foreword is written by Vice President Hubert Humphrey.

Bill had worked for the Red Cross for many years. He was from the Bronx in New York. He spoke so fast and with such an accent, I could barely understand a word he was saying—especially when he got excited telling one of his many tales. His specialty was what he called "instant hospitals." He could put up a packaged, portable surgery center in hours. It was supplied with everything needed for medical emergencies. He loved going out in the middle of nowhere under the worst possible circumstances, and setting these in place.

LANGUAGE AND CULTURE

Al didn't warn me that my trips in and out of Tan Son Nhut airport would not be typical. To avoid rockets, the planes took-off and landed as fast and as close to vertical as possible. The groaning and straining of the plane as it suddenly dropped for a landing—and left your stomach somewhere in the clouds—was a thrill I could have done without. To make matters worse, the commercial flights into Saigon from Manila were on Air France, nicknamed Air Chance. Not a comforting thought.

Evenings were not typical either. After the six o'clock night curfew, anything moving in the Saigon River that ran through town was fired upon. You could hear the pop, pop, pop all night long. At times they were firing at dead bodies floating down from the north. There was barbed wire concertina everywhere. Machine gun nests decorated street corners. At night, Al and I would sit on the roof of the apartment building and watch the war. Flashes of light twenty-five miles away were from B52 raids. The booms that followed rocked the building.

Bob, Al's roommate, became interested in the Chieu Hoi program. Leaflets and messages with incentives to defect were sent to Viet Cong soldiers. Any who took advantage of the program were called Hoi Chanh. Bob, who had one glass eye and horrible vision, would slosh around in rice paddies at night with our soldiers. Forgetting it was dangerous, he would stand up and call (in fluent Vietnamese) to Viet Cong to defect. Why he wasn't used for target practice is a mystery.

The USO welcomed military. Soldiers had to unload their weapons into a barrel of sand near the front door before entering the building. One day during a monsoon rain, Al and I were walking by when a Sergeant fired his gun into the barrel—and then dropped it onto the pavement. We heard a loud crack as it fired on impact. The crowds on the sidewalk dropped to the ground. I felt Al's arms dragging me down into the muddy water of the trash-filled gutter. Luckily that bullet missed everyone. Lying in that gutter is a memory I will never forget.

Saigon is actually a pretty city, if you overlook the hundreds and hundreds of Honda motorcycles, huge baskets of cooked cockroaches for sale on the sidewalks, muddy alleys, and military presence. Many of the streets are lined with huge Flame Trees that create an umbrella of spectacular red-orange flowers. The flower market spreads color and fragrance over a city block. Vietnamese women in their flowing silk AoDai grace the sidewalks. Groups of young female students scurry along in uniforms that belong in a *Madeline* book. Buddhist monks in saffron robes dot the streets. Men pedal their passengers in cyclos, a bicycle rickshaw.

A custom that seemed strange at first was to see men holding hands on the street. Affection between men and women or between women is never shown publicly, but it is common between men. Love is openly declared. Al had three Vietnamese male friends that cared for him and helped him in so many ways. Knopp, a the guard at his building, would protect Al's apartment and stay there when Al was in the Philippines. Ho, a monk who claimed to be President Ho Chi Mihn's grandson, loved to visit, and Le Chan Vu was a young student who took Al into areas of Saigon that were on no city tour. After Al left Saigon, Le Chan Vu sent us a beautiful note. It was almost a tender love letter. Unfortunately, we found out later that he was Viet Cong.

French influence is everywhere. There is lingerie to rival anything Victoria's Secret can muster. Some of the younger girls wear a sheer AoDai which displays the lacy bras. French restaurants serve wonderful meals.

> **Point of interest:** Public dancing was not permitted. There were a few restaurants with a speak-easy atmosphere that allowed performers to dance.

French, the diplomatic language, is spoken on the street. The only Vietnamese words I learned was *di di*, go away, *Ba*, older woman, and *Chua Oi*, omigosh. The vendors all knew "number one" was the best and "number ten" the worst. Ba, Al's maid and superb cook, could speak Vietnamese, French, Laotian, and pretty good English with no education. She made me feel dense.

PROTOCOL AND ETIQUETTE

Wives, including Ambassador Laise of Nepal, wife of Ambassador Bunker, were allowed to visit Vietnam from the various safe-havens only when the Embassy sent out a notice that it was "safe." On one of our visits, Ambassador Laise announced a reception for any wife in-country. Unless you were contagious or dying, you accepted any invitation to the Embassy or the Residence.

My leather heels were covered in mud from running around Saigon. (Remember the USO gutter?) They needed to be polished for the visit the next day. Al told me to leave them outside the bedroom door for the maid to clean. The next morning both my shoes and the maid were gone. We found out later she thought they were a gift and took them to sell. The only other shoes I had were rubber flip-flops. There was no time to buy any other.

I dressed and called for an Embassy car and driver. It turned out, so had every other visiting wife in Saigon. None was available. Al was allowed one vehicle in Saigon. The Embassy gave him a motorcycle while he was waiting for a jeep. We couldn't find a taxi, so I climbed up side-saddle on the bright yellow motorcycle in my fancy dress, hat, gloves, and rubber flip-flops. I hung on for dear life through Saigon traffic, which is fender to fender Honda motorcycles, beat up taxis, and jay-walking pedestrians. The Marine guard at the Embassy tried to keep a straight face as he helped me off my perch. I must have looked pretty silly.

Ambassador Laise graciously ignored my bare feet in the flip-flops, but there were some sidelong stares. I found an Embassy driver to take me back to the apartment after what seemed like a very long reception.

YOU BUY ME SAIGON TEA?

In Vietnam, the girls in the bars were sometimes prostitutes, but surprisingly, many were not. They hung around the customers and urged them to buy drinks. Their come-on was, "You buy me Saigon Tea?" I have no idea why, but I wanted to see how that worked. The right occasion came when Al and I were joined by three of his associates for dinner; Tom from USAID, Bill from GAO, and Marty from World Health. I had four male escorts.

We walked into a bar on TuDo Street. I was the only Caucasian woman in the place. Two pretty girls wearing the traditional silk AoDai, led us to a booth that held all seven of us. We were trying to be inconspicuous, but Al somehow caught his foot on a bar stool. If anyone had missed us coming in the door, they certainly knew we were there when the stool crashed to the floor.

I can only remember the name of one of the girls. Kim and her friend took an instant liking to Tom. He was about twenty-five years old, slender, and very nice looking. He had a baby-face and almost no beard. The girls kept rubbing his chin. My guess is that they liked his chin because Vietnamese men have little body hair. A clue might also be the nickname in Vietnam for the more hairy American men. The word means bear.

Vietnamese women are tiny, delicate, and finely featured. Their AoDai accents every curve. If American women had known how exquisite the Vietnamese women were, they would have been a lot more worried about their men over there.

> **Point of interest:** The Vietnamese nickname for American women is trau nuoc which means water buffalo. Draw your own conclusions.

Both girls spoke very good English—and neither asked the men to buy them Saigon Tea. Actually, we three women sat and jabbered and the men were almost ignored. I asked a lot of questions about their traditional dress and they volunteered to take me to the Central Market to buy silk to have one made. I was surprised when Al thought it would be okay. We made a date for the next morning.

The two of them arrived on their Honda motorcycle about 10:00 a.m. Three on a motorcycle in the insane Saigon traffic didn't seem like a good idea, even though it was not unusual to see whole families on a single Honda. I convinced them that a taxi would be better, especially if I paid for it.

The taxi wound its way through hundreds of motorcycles to finally stop at the open-air Central Market. I began to wish I had not stepped into that taxi. I had no idea where I was and American women could easily become a commodity worth thousands of dollars. They could have been taking me to a Viet Cong around any corner. I didn't know it until the next day, but Al had made arrangements for Knopp, the guard at his building, to follow me. Knopp could have lost his job for leaving his post, but he went anyway. He called Al all during the day to let him know that I was still okay. I would have felt better had I known Knopp was right behind me.

Even with all the worry, I had a wonderful day. We bought gorgeous silk at the market. Next was a tiny little tailor shop at the end of a dark and scary alley. The AoDai flows freely from the waist over silk pants, yet I was measured in twenty-seven different places. No wonder they fit so perfectly.

I am absolutely, positively sure our lunch restaurant was not on any tourist list. Kim ordered a wonderful soup with noodles, *Pho*, (fuh) and something like an egg roll, *Cha Gio* (Chaw yah). The Cha Gio were large with hard, slick sides and simply would not stay between my chopsticks. I finally gave up when I discovered I could stab the things with one chopstick and pick it up. The girls thought it was hilarious. They told almost everyone in the restaurant, so we all shared in the joke. It was good-hearted fun, but I made it a point to learn how to use chopsticks soon after that. After lunch, they took me back to the apartment. Two days later they took me back to the tailor shop to pick up my new clothes.

I learned a lot about the two of them. They came from huge families in the province and had been sent by their fathers to Saigon to earn money for the family. Maybe they had me fooled, but I honestly do not think they slept with anyone as part of their job. Interestingly, they wouldn't let me pay for anything except the taxi and what I bought at the market. Lunch was their treat. I bought them each a gift and had to practically force it on them. I hope I didn't pull some cultural blunder.

What was left of Al's Class room

Refugee Camp

The AoDai

MANILA, PHILIPPINES TO LAGOS, NIGERIA

February 1970

We flew to our new Post in Nigeria. There were some stops along the way.

BANGKOK, THAILAND

Al was transferred to Nigeria. He would arrive in Manila a few days early and we would travel together. That sounds like a simple plan, but travel overseas can be risky. A decision had to be made whether to split up the kids and travel on separate planes or on one. The logic is, at least one parent has to survive any disaster.

It was a marvelous opportunity for a trip. We planned to visit friends in Thailand, to see Bombay (now Mumbai), India, and to visit a game reserve in Nairobi. We had reservations at the Ngong House. It is famous for its tree houses on stilts where wild animals wandered around beneath you. We could hardly wait.

Just days before we left, the Nigerian government pulled the visas for everyone but Al. We were to have been the first family allowed in after the end of the Biafra War. Someone changed his mind.

Nigeria is a small country. Their diplomats often work in borrowed space in larger embassies. The nearest Nigerian consulate on our route was in the British Embassy in Rome. Our much anticipated trip to the game reserve was cancelled. We packed up our shorts, sandals, bathing suits, and the cat, and headed for Rome in the bitterly cold month of February.

It took two of us to give our cat, Nako, half of the Valium pill the vet said would put her to sleep. It took three of us to get her four legs in a Pan Am pet carrier. We checked our twenty-one suitcases and boarded a plane headed for the first stop, Thailand.

> **Note:** We named the cat Nako because she kept climbing on the furniture and breaking things. We could hear the maids', "ay nako'" which means Omigod. It became a trend. We had cats named "Choi oi", omigod in Vietnamese and "chunche," Spanish for junk or stuff.

Half way to Bangkok, the cat went nuts. She mewed—no, wailed—and nearly scratched and gouged the carrier to pieces. We gave her the other half of the Valium. I swear, that made it worse. We didn't know what to do, so we gave her another half. We figured it would either calm her down or kill her. By this time, the carrier was useless and the cat was in my lap. How we got her off the plane, through Customs, and into another carrier without having to chase her through the airport, I don't know. At times she had all four legs stiff against my chest and the only thing I had half a grip on, was one paw. She never did calm down, although now she yawned once in awhile.

The few days in Thailand were fun. Al worked with a man in Vietnam whose wife was safe-havened in Bangkok. They gave a dinner party for us to meet other USAID families. We had little time, so although Al hates guided tours, we climbed aboard a bus that took us to magnificent Thai and Cambodian temples and immense Buddhist statues made of gold. (Did you know that King Bhumibol was born in Cambridge Massachusetts? His father was a Harvard student.)

Bangkok is a city of countless waterways called klongs. Little huts selling produce, gems, clothing, and silk line the edge. Industrious vendors fill their tiny boats with goods and travel the klongs as miniature floating markets. Water taxis are everywhere.

Our kids blond hair attracted a lot of attention. Crowds, especially children, would gather and surround them. The kids rode an elephant and fed a bear on the dock. We bought some beautiful silk and a set of bronze tableware for twelve which we dragged with us on the plane. That box of tableware weighed at least thirty pounds.

We attracted crowds

Klong waterway

Temple

MUMBAI, INDIA

We landed around three o'clock in the morning in Bombay (now Mumbai). It took forever for the Customs agents to go through our twenty-one suitcases and release the cat. Exhausted, we just wanted to get to the hotel. A new problem arose. The tiny taxis held only two people and a few suitcases. We had no choice but to take three separate taxis. No bus ran at that hour.

Butch and Jim climbed into one taxi. Al took Ken, and I had Janice, with Eric on my lap. We asked, begged, and paid, the drivers to stay together. It made no difference once we left the airport. I didn't see either of the other taxis as we drove for thirty minutes down dark, dismal streets. People were sleeping on newspapers on the sidewalks. I didn't know if we headed for the hotel or white slavery. It is hard to describe the relief I felt to finally see the Taj Mahal Palace Hotel and the rest of the family. I was a wreck and we had just arrived.

> **Note of interest:** The Taj Mahal Palace is an extraordinarily beautiful and luxurious five-star hotel with 565 rooms. It was viciously attacked in 2008 by terrorists. One hundred and sixty-seven people were killed. Sadly, a good portion of the hotel was bombed and set on fire.

Al worked with a man from India whose wife lived in Bombay. He had asked us to deliver some things to her. We rented a car and driver and set off to find her. The car was running in spurts, so we stopped at a gas station. As Al and the driver were working behind the open hood, an enormous crowd pushed in around the passenger windows. They pressed their faces against the glass. We rolled up the windows, but the car became an oven in the intense heat. Al saw what was going on and rescued us.

We finally got on our way. The driver let us out to walk through some pathways behind an apartment building. We stepped around a man we thought was sleeping on the sidewalk. Two men in an ox-cart pulled up and dragged off his dead body as we watched. What a sad, sad, place.

We were carried to the third floor of the apartment building in a groaning, wobbly elevator. The woman wasn't home so we waited and talked with her parents and her brother. They shared the rooms. Her brother was a radical communist who entertained us with stories about how his country should be run and the mistakes that Americans made. When the woman got home, she took us to the wonderful botanical gardens near the harbor. Janice and one of the boys got on the tallest teeter-totter I ever saw. Somehow, her brother got off when Janice was at the highest point and she came crashing down like a rock. My heart stood still. She seemed okay, but couldn't breathe or talk to tell us if she was hurt. All I could think of was, "If this had to happen, why did it have to happen in India?" She was fine, but we all had a real scare.

Next, we had dinner at a popular restaurant. It was luxuriously furnished and the waiters were in uniform. The ambiance was deceiving. It was unnerving to have to pick up our feet so the cockroaches didn't run over our shoes. We didn't eat much.

Bombay was an odd place. Residents were literally starving to death. There were huge Brahmas wandering around in the streets. They are considered sacred and allowed to go anywhere. I wondered how many people that animal could feed. Not too sanitary either.

We wandered around and shopped the next day. Al bought a silk sari with silver threads for me. I bought some brass pieces and some fun things for the kids. Al and I decided to eat dinner alone at the hotel that night. The front desk sent up a giant Sheik to baby-sit. He looked like a six-foot-six walking wall. When it was too late, we found out that his idea of baby-sitting was to stand outside the room door with his arms crossed.

Homeless

Brahma on the Street

TEL AVIV, ISRAEL

I had always wanted to travel to Egypt and Israel. The political atmosphere at the time would not allow anyone to travel from one country to the other. We had to opt for one or the other. We chose Israel.

As we prepared to land, the stewardess announced that the passengers should take the crash position and lean forward on a pillow. The landing was smooth as glass. Nothing happened, except that she scared everyone to death. Strange. When we landed, we taxied to a place on the tarmac away from the airport and just sat there. Awfully strange.

Soon, anyone with residence in Israel was taken off the plane. Even more strange. We waited. A bus pulled up. Five men armed with carbine rifles and dressed in heavy, black overcoats, boarded our plane. They had stern and serious expressions, and no sense of humor. Each passenger was asked to stand in the aisle as they performed a seat to seat search, checking overheads and seat pockets. After nearly an hour of a very somber search, the captain came down the aisle and told the men he was running behind schedule and needed permission to fly. They ignored him.

Finally, one of the men announced that no one else would be allowed off the plane. If you were going somewhere other than the plane's next destination in Greece, you would be transferred by bus to another plane. Then they left.

So much for our trip to the Holy Land. The airline did give us first class seats on the way to Greece since we were "inconvenienced" in Tel Aviv. It didn't make up for the lost sites, but was a treat. Once we were in the air, we were told that someone had blown up a plane headed for Tel Aviv. The men had been searching for a bomb.

ATHENS, GREECE AND ROME, ITALY

We had great plans for Greece. We wanted to see all the tourist sites. We landed in a virtual downpour. It was the middle of the morning and it was cold, windy, dark, and just plain nasty. We checked the weather report. If anything, it was predicted to get worse. We ate lunch, shopped in the airport gift shops, and debated what to do. We had only two days to spend in Greece so we decided to go on to Rome where the weather was supposed to be considerably better. Another missed opportunity.

It was still very cold in Rome, but it was clear and crisp. With our thin tropical blood and summer clothes, we were not ready for a European February. We checked into the El Presidente Hotel near the Coliseum. The British Embassy was trying to help us with the visa problem. Nigeria was accepting Al's visa, but refused to re-issue to the rest of us. We were told it might take a week to get new visas. We thought we would take the cat out from time to time.

While we were getting settled, Al went downtown to buy a harness and leash. He put the tropical cat down on the European ice-cold sidewalk. It was out of the guaranteed-to-hold harness in a split second. We spent the next ten days making daily trips to the underground parking garage with pieces of bacon saying, "Here kitty, kitty." We never did find that cat. Hopefully, it found its way to the vendor shops around the Coliseum that fed scraps to the plump cats that hung around. When we left, Nako became an illegal immigrant to Italy.

The first order of business was to buy winter coats and shoes. Once warm, we rented a tiny Fiat and visited all the wonderful sites. We spent hours in the Vatican art galleries and worked our way back to the Sistine Chapel, Michelangelo's masterpiece. It was just minutes before one o'clock when we got to the chapel. Kenny had a problem with the Tropical Sprue in that, when he had to go, he had to go right then. He couldn't wait and the doors closed at one o'clock that day. I asked the magnificently dressed Vatican guard if he would wait a few minutes and let us in. I must have looked pretty sad, because he agreed to wait and let me take Kenny to the bathroom some distance away.

Because it was after hours, we were the only people in that beautiful chapel. There we were, alone with Michelangelo, and not a sound. It is a memory I will always cherish. I still get teary-eyed when I think of it.

Saint Peter's Cathedral is exquisite beyond description. And the Pieta takes your breath away. Mary would be over seven feet tall if she stood. She is a gentle giant, cradling her fallen son in her arms. Art is everywhere and each piece is more beautiful than the last.

Al had to check with the Embassy each day for the status of the visas, so we could only sight-see within a day's drive. We experimented in restaurants, visited the catacombs, the Forum, the Coliseum, the Apian Way and many more wonderful places. The Church of Santa Maria has the Bocca della Verita (Mouth of Truth), an enormous flat stone head of a God with an open mouth. According to legend, it was used during the Middle Ages as a trial by ordeal. If you were lying and put your hand in the mouth, it would bite off your hand. An executioner would hide behind the stone with a sword, ready to strike. It was fun to watch the kids gingerly insert their hands and jerk them out.

Butch went native. Many street corners had little coffee shops that served you on the sidewalk. People gathered there for a quick warm-up and conversation. What we didn't know is that you could request something a little stronger than cream and sugar in your coffee. Butch took a strong liking to those coffee shops.

We visited the Fountain of Trevi several times. It is said that if you toss a coin in the fountain and make a wish, it will come true. Butch and Janice wished to come back to Rome. They did eventually return.

Every day, we ate breakfast at the hotel. Stephan, our waiter, adopted us. He made it his goal in life to feed us a great breakfast. He heard about our cat and took the kids down to the garage with food scraps, trying to find Nako, every day. We bought him a leather-covered wine decanter as a good-bye gift. He actually cried.

Eric picked up a germ somewhere and started throwing up. When he felt a little better we decided to drive to Anzio. We stopped for lunch in a small town with a plaza and a few buildings. The hotel restaurant was a gathering place where little groups sat around and chatted. No one spoke English and they didn't understand our attempt at Italian or our Spanish, so we had trouble ordering. They brought out someone from the lobby who spoke German. That didn't help. Butch and Eric hadn't learned German yet.

We couldn't seem to get the order across to the waitress, so we decided everyone in Italy must know what minestrone was and ordered it. They didn't know the word. Everyone in the restaurant was involved by now. And everyone was having a good laugh. I finally went with the waitress into the kitchen and met the cook.

The kitchen held an ancient four-burner household stove. With a lot of laughing and hand signaling, we found a big kettle, dumped in meat and vegetables from the equally ancient refrigerator, added some home-made pasta and made a terrific pot of minestrone. We were all having such a good time that we stayed all afternoon.

Note: We discovered that when you ordered spaghetti in Rome that was exactly what you got—no sauce on the pasta of any kind. Pizza did not resemble anything we make in the States, and Wimpie's hamburgers were just awful.

Speaking of spaghetti, Al and I hired a baby-sitter and ventured out one night for dinner alone. The waiter who served us spaghetti was an artist. He raised the pasta several times into the air in spectacular patterns with such emotion that we still talk about it. That night too, was the first time I was served fruit and cheese as a dessert. It tasted almost as good as pie and coffee.

We got word that the visas were ready. We waited hours and hours at the airport for our British Airways flight to Nigeria. They finally told us the plane had crashed-landed in London and they had to prepare another aircraft for our flight. We finally boarded the new plane and headed for our next home. A large part of the flight was hours of nothing below but the white sand of the Sahara Desert. It is hard to describe that immense expanse. We finally landed in Lagos.

Mouth of Truth bites your hand if you lie

Fountain of Trevi

LAGOS, NIGERIA

March 1970 to April 1971

I'm glad I had the experience of the Nigerian Post, but it was pretty scary at times.

A NEW WAY OF LIFE

Traveling with Official passports, Customs officers typically showed us the courtesy of minimal inspection. In Nigeria, four tables were over-flowing with our twenty-one suitcases and the four cardboard boxes containing souvenirs, tableware for twelve, and full set of crystal glassware. The Embassy aide who met us tried to intervene, but the officers just became irritated and deliberately slowed down their search. After they had stirred everything, it didn't all fit back into the suitcases and boxes. We stuffed the leftovers in trash bags and left. The parking lot had no lights. We did the best we could in the dark to cram the seven of us, the aide, the driver, and all the suitcases and boxes into the Embassy station wagon. It was late. We were tired. We were hungry.

A couple of blocks beyond the airport fence, our driver pointed out flashlight beams. Soldiers flagged us down. Suddenly, the barrel of a carbine rifle brushed inches from my nose and then back out the window. This was our introduction to the Nigerian military. Most of us had to get out of the car in order to spread out every suitcase, box and garbage bag in the dirt along the road. One soldier held a flashlight while another stirred each item once again. By the time we loaded up and got on our way, we had serious doubts about the decision to accept a Post in Nigeria.

Lagos Lagoon shares its name with the city of Lagos which means "lakes" in Portuguese. A better translation would be swamp. The marshy swamp is more than fifty kilometers long and thirteen kilometers wide and empties into the ocean via the harbor. A main channel runs through the middle of the city with branches here and there. If I described it right, you are picturing water everywhere—and what goes with water? Humidity. The air was so unbelievably heavy it made us queasy. We all had that "I'm coming down with the flu" feeling for days.

Our two storied, four-bedroom house on Raymond Najoko Street off Awolowa Road was actually very nice, but in typical third-world fashion, things were missing or not functioning. The house was surrounded by a wall with an iron gate across the driveway. A screened porch upstairs between two of the bedrooms gave us a good view of the constant parade of colorful characters that walked to and from the open-air market at the end of the street. Many had huge, tall loads on their heads.

The driveway created a little bridge as it ran over an open, narrow cement channel that was the Nigerian version of a sewer system. It was common to see both men and women with a leg on each side of the channel and chatting while relieving themselves. More serious business required a squatting position, but that was usually children. During the rainy season, debris would build up in the channel and not pass under the driveway bridges. Men would come by and offer to clear it for a dash.

The dash was a tip or a bribe and was the basic way to get anything done on the street or in the government. Our garbage cans would be tipped over by huge rats. A dash would get the mess cleaned up. My mother sent us a package through the regular mail system. The Embassy let us know it was hung up in Customs and there was a large tariff due. It cost us a dash and an $11.00 discounted tariff to get the package cleared through Customs. The liquor and agriculture tax was on a fruitcake!

> **Note:** We sent and received mail through the Embassy pouch. Packages were difficult as we were allowed a limit of only one pound per package. I remember Mother having to mail a pair of pajamas in two separate packages due to the weight.

It was really scary in Nigeria to watch my children being picked up for school every morning in an Embassy station wagon with the back door lowered to accommodate the armed escort with a loaded M2 carbine rifle. I thank God he never had to fire that gun.

The American school was next door to a Nigerian military facility. The kids constantly complained about the soldiers running through the school grounds, scaring everyone and stealing the canteens of fresh water we sent them to school with every day. We complained to the school and the Embassy, but it fell on deaf ears. Janice told me years later that they drank from the fountain even though the water wasn't potable at the school.

Some of the teachers were not as good as they were in the Philippines. Janice had one in particular that kept lowering her marks for errors in grammar which weren't errors at all. We had to review all her papers to be sure she was being graded properly.

Our sponsors in Lagos hired Bassie, our cook, and Sunday, our Small Boy. Bassie was a small-framed, spunky five-foot, three-inch Hausa. He insisted on wearing white uniforms that a prior employer had bought for him. He wore either no shoes or rubber flip flops and looked all in the world like a miniature, barefoot milkman. Most of what he cooked was very British, but he learned what we liked very quickly. He turned me into a lifetime fan of Shepherd's pie—after he took the white pepper out of it. It nearly set us on fire the first time we tried it.

Sunday was seventeen-years old and Bassie's "circumcision brother." Anyone who was circumcised in the same ceremony with you had to be allowed access to your home, your wealth, your food, and your wife (or wives). Nice thought, but you can see where that might be a thorny problem with a lazy or demanding "brother." Unfortunately, that happened all too often.

Sunday was a very handsome young man. He was a little taller than Bassie and well built. He was Bassie's helper, but his primary responsibility was the laundry. So near to the equator, the sun baked your clothes and took the color out very quickly. Anything folded over the line easily took on a white line on the fold, so clothes had to be hung up and taken down as soon as they were dry. This certainly didn't take very long. Nasty little tse tse flies just loved to embed themselves and lay eggs in anything hanging on a clothesline. Once on your skin, the tse tse buries itself and lays eggs in a big boil-like pocket. They transmit diseases that kill thousands each year. Ironing or a clothes dryer will kill the eggs. Sunday had to hand-wash the laundry and carefully iron everything including towels, sheets, socks, and underwear until the washer and dryer arrived months later.

Sunday wanted very much to learn to read. The kids and I spent hours with him and he did very well. We were all very proud of him. And I was very proud of the kids. We all got such a kick out his progress.

Electricity overseas is almost always 220v. American-made appliances had to be plugged into a converter which didn't always work. The smell of hot metal meant you had burned up another appliance. I remember trying to change a light bulb in a floor lamp and accidentally touched metal. I had to pick myself up off the marble floor. 220v is a big jolt.

Electricity built up in appliances, especially in the kitchen. We heard stories that a small child of a USAID family touched metal on a refrigerator door with no shoes on and actually died.

Al and I liked to have coffee after dinner in the living room. We made coffee in an electric percolator in those days. The electricity would build up in the pot and give you quite a shock if you were unfortunate enough to touch the metal. Even though we were constantly reminding Bassie to put on his rubber flip flops, he inevitably would go into the kitchen without shoes and pick up the pot. We would watch him go through the door and wait a minute or two and the—also inevitable—shriek would come. It reminded me of the old Goofy cartoons where he would let out his famous yell as he was falling down a mountain.

Justine, an Igbo nineteen-year old, was hired later as a nanny. The Igbo are very large, dark, and strong. Justine was husky and easily six feet tall, but sweet and gentle. Kidnapping was always a very real threat for Americans, especially for those with blonde hair and blue eyes. Justine went everywhere with the three younger kids as a chaperone. Nigerians believe that if you eat the part that you admire of someone, you take on those qualities. If they were smart—you ate their brain. You watched your kids like a hawk.

> **Note:** Bassie said it was possible to buy "long meat" at the JuJu (black magic) market. Long meat is human flesh.

Almost no one, except Americans, used deodorant or shaved their legs or under their arms. Climbing into an elevator with no air-conditioning and a crowd of Nigerians took courage. It was easy to pick out the Europeans at the swimming pool. At times you could smell Justine before you could see her. When the kids started complaining, I decided to say something to her. It was really a hard thing to do, but I bought her some deodorant and explained the problem. She seemed to understand and did use it from then on. I always wondered what she thought. I remember one our neighbors who was from Germany told me that "Americans were so antiseptic that not even their cheese stank."

I was called Madame and Justine seemed fine with taking instruction from me. The two men always wanted to refer everything to Al, the Master, which translates as "teacher." If my instructions had to do with something in the house, it was okay—but not good. Women are chattel in Nigeria. A man can have as many wives as he wishes. However there is an unwritten rule that it really is "as many wives as he can afford." They sure weren't wild about my being in charge.

The level of education is pitiful. Bassie and Justine had no formal education at all. I think Sunday had a year or two. It also was a problem for us. If I wanted to leave a note, no one could read it. I finally got Sunday to understand what S, M, and L meant when he was sorting clothes. Pictures on canned goods and boxes identified the pantry goods. I discovered they had amazing memories. I could send them to the store with a verbal grocery list and they would remember every item, no matter how long the list.

Numbers were another story. They could tell you to the shilling exactly how much money they were owed on payday or how much change they had coming at the market. I'm not sure I ever figured out the currency. The money was in pence, shillings, pounds, and crowns. It was in denominations of six, twelve, twenty and twenty-one instead of five, ten, and twenty. I probably was cheated occasionally.

Payroll in all of the countries had to paid in cash. There always had to be exactly the right amount in an envelope for each person each week. We used the Embassy for ninety-five percent of our banking. Actually, the only "banking" we did was to get either dollars or local currency. We kept a Stateside account for anything we paid for in the United States or at the Embassy. There was no such thing as a local check. Credit cards were a new idea at that time. You were always conscious of how much cash you were carrying. You didn't want too much or you could be robbed. You always needed enough for gas, groceries, market purchases, or restaurants in local currency, plus that weekly payroll.

When we first arrived, Bassie's wife had just delivered their first child. He moved them into the servant's quarters in the backyard. We almost never heard that baby cry. She must have been a very good mother. Their house wasn't much. It was molded and looked like a child's plastic play house. There were no doors to close, only rectangular openings. You had to step over a little edge to go through each opening. There were molded flat places to sit or lie on. I hated that thing. I have no idea if they considered it a good or bad place to live. I have always regretted not talking to them more about it. Sunday and Justine stayed in it too. The Embassy assured me it was a nice place, but I felt guilty. They had friends come by to visit from time to time. Since their house was on the far side of our backyard, we often saw strangers wandering down the driveway. Bassie was careful not to overdo.

One day, Bassie came running into the house in a panic. He told me the baby couldn't go to the bathroom. I decided it would be better to ask his wife what the problem was, so went out to their house. The baby was crying his little heart out. When I put my hands on his tummy, it was as hard as a rock. His mother had the strangest reaction when I touched him. She seemed to be afraid. I gave Bassie a lot of instructions and a bottle of Karo syrup to loosen the little guy up. He seemed to be fine the next day.

Water for the bathrooms was collected in two cisterns on the roof, just above each bath tub. One stormy night, we came home from a movie to find a waterfall coming down the stairs from the second floor. Al ran to the kitchen and got a huge butcher knife to poke holes in both bathroom ceilings so water would pour into the bath tub. That relieved the pressure enough that the ceiling wouldn't collapse, but then it looked like Niagara Falls. We called the Embassy for a maintenance man and they said it would have to wait until morning. We slept on the living room chairs and sofa and the one bedroom downstairs.

Everything in every upstairs room was soaked. The clothes and shoes in the closets were wet. Cases of paper goods stored upstairs were wet. Some of the furniture was wet. At least the beds escaped. It didn't take long for things to dry in that heat; however, we didn't expect the mold that appeared in iridescent lime-green and gold. It grew and grew and covered the walls, the floor, and anything that had been wet. To tell you the truth, it was actually kind of pretty, but all ten of us had to pitch in to clean up the mess. The washer and dryer ran for days. Shoes and the furniture were never quite the same.

WHAT DADDY DID AT HIS NIGERIAN OFFICE

Protocol for the wives in the Nigerian Mission was almost non-existent. If there were social functions, we missed them. Al worked with Ambassador Trueheart, but his wife stayed in the background.

Al was in charge of the Health Program, one of the largest projects there. A child's birth is not registered in Nigeria until they are three months old because they often do not live that long. Measles and Small Pox were the big killers. Because of the dark color of the native skin, it was common to see someone with obvious white scars all over their body.

It was difficult to protect against the disease due to the superstition and lack of education. Teams would go into the bush to vaccinate in a village and arrive to find it completely deserted. The villagers would hide.

One of his most interesting projects was to design a four-page brochure to educate the population regarding the benefits of vaccination. It took some creative thought because it had to be done without text. His audience could not read.

> **Note:** The village chief was called Oba. An Oba was entitled to many wives. Al was invited to a village to witness an Oba take his twenty-sixth wife. It was a fascinating day, but the ceremony included the sacrifice of a live goat. I couldn't watch the struggling animal as they ever so slowly sawed its neck.

One of the reasons we left Nigeria, aside from the health problems Kenny was having, was an incident that infuriated Al. It was decided that the Health Program needed over one hundred new trucks. Al did all the paperwork for the purchase. He refused to sign the purchase order though because there was an entire field literally full of trucks that had only some minor things wrong with them. Al couldn't see paying for new trucks when all those trucks were just sitting there. He got called on the carpet by the Ambassador. I give him credit though. He stood his ground. It was wrong to spend all that money on new trucks when most of the trucks sitting in that field could have been easily and inexpensively repaired.

We have found, in almost all the third world countries that the word "maintenance" isn't in their vocabulary. That probably accounts for most of the run-down look that you see everywhere. These vehicles were just parked when they didn't "work" anymore.

LANGUAGE AND CULTURE

Although there are over three hundred different ethnic groups in Nigeria, the main tribes are the Igbo in the southeast, the Hausa-Fulani in the north, and the Yoruba in the southwest near Lagos. The Nigerian civil war was a political conflict caused by the attempted secession of the southeastern provinces to form the Republic of Biafra. The war was supposed to be over, but I'm not sure the Nigerians were aware of it yet.

The war made headlines all over the world. Horrible pictures of starving babies were appearing in newspapers and on magazine covers. The Nigerian solution to that publicity was to outlaw cameras and arrest anyone caught taking pictures.

> **Note:** The stories were true about starving babies, but the reason was not necessarily the war. Tribal rules say that the older and wiser tribesmen should be fed first. If there wasn't enough food left for the babies—oh well.

We couldn't buy film, take a photo, or develop film. We did manage to literally sneak around one day and took a few pictures on the one roll of film we had with us. Sadly, we have almost no photographs of our African Post.

Nigeria had been a British colony, so English was spoken. Each tribe had its own unique language. The different tribes couldn't speak to each other, so tended to use English. The Yoruba men wore wonderful robes and little round, embroidered hats. You could spot the men educated in Great Britain. In addition to the traditional robe they sported a bowler hat, shiny wristwatch, and a black umbrella. Many wore African patterned, silk-screened shirts. Strangely though, the fabric was actually made in the Netherlands (of all places), and wasn't African at all—like the Afro haircut that was so popular in the States. I never saw that in Africa either.

The women most often wore plain cotton blouses with short sleeves, a collar-less neckline, and a colorful wrap-around floor-length skirt. There was nothing plain however, about the large, elaborate head-ties. They were folded into intricate patterns that symbolized marital status and special occasions.

The colonial British were hated. Unfortunately, we looked just like them. It was very unpleasant to be disliked for no apparent reason, but the experience makes it much easier to understand how some minorities feel. For us it was temporary, but for them it is a life-long ordeal. The prejudice manifested itself in things as simple as taxi fare. There were no meters, so you had to negotiate before you got in the taxi. Our white skin always caused the rate to rise.

We were in Lagos only a short time before we found we didn't like the Brits very much either. We lived on Ikoyi Island and were going to dinner in a hotel (a little safer to eat in) restaurant on the mainland. As we approached the door, a Nigerian and a Brit tried to enter about the same time. When the Nigerian didn't step aside, the Brit threatened to hit him with a walking stick and called him a "bloody baboon." Al grabbed that man's arm and stopped him. Now the Brit had to tangle with Al. He backed off, but glared at us all through dinner.

Bassie had worked for a Brit before he worked for us who must have been a real winner. Bassie just assumed that we were going to abuse him. There was only one dry-cleaner in the whole city and it was nowhere near us. Bassie decided to hand-wash Al's hand-tailored wool and silk suit and hang it over the line to dry. He left it on the line too long and a white line formed where the suit was folded over the clothesline. Bassie showed Al the suit—and handed him a long bamboo reed he had cut from the back yard. He wanted to know if "Master wanted to beat him now?" Al was ready to strangle him, but felt sorry for him at the same time.

Ikoyi Island was where all the prominent people lived. Many of the best homes were a combination Embassy or Consulate and Residence for an Ambassador representing a small country. We were surrounded by embassies from Pakistan, Israel, Iran, and other countries. A little different atmosphere than your normal neighborhood.

The Yugoslavian Embassy was next door. When we moved in, they painted all the windows along the side of the house facing us white so that we couldn't see in. Because Yugoslavia was a communist-bloc country, we were supposed to report all conversations with them to our Embassy. That was ridiculous because they had kids that played with our kids every day. Our Embassy finally backed down and said just "important conversations." One of their little boys, about eight years old, told me that when people did things he didn't like, he could "step on them." I wondered if he heard that from his father.

There were superstitions about everything. I spent pleasant hours bargaining and chatting with hawkers on my doorstep. They would tell me stories about the wood carvings and items they carried on their heads or pulled in little, hand-made carts. The craftsmen made wonderful miniature carvings out of milk, brown, or pink colored thorns that are cut from Ata or Egungun trees. They depict Nigerian life and activities.

There was a carved god for just about everything from fertility to small pox. Many of the carvings were "painted" with shoe polish and smelled like it. Most items were very simple, but a few were elaborately and exquisitely carved and finished. Ancestors lingered in trees and in the bush and would be called by the carvings to either help or hurt you. You had to watch your step.

Point of interest: If you were bored on Sundays, you could take a quick run to Port Harcourt to watch the public hangings. Vigilante groups added to the entertainment at times by beheading and burning their victims. Nigerian police did try to stop them.

The lack of prejudice among the kids was remarkable. Most of the State Department kids had been raised overseas in countries all over the world and didn't seem to realize that they were all different. It was wonderful to see them just be friends with every color and nationality. Wouldn't it be something if the whole world could be like that?

GROCERY SHOPPING 104-106

In Nigeria, very little food was safe. Milk was often tubercular. We found out after eating it for a few weeks, that the mysterious crunch in the store-bought bread was actually rat or mouse feces. I still gag when I think of it. The popcorn at the theaters was extra crunchy for the same reason. With five kids and no bread available, coming up with lunch menus became a challenge.

Sanitation: There wasn't any. Meats hung out in the open at both the open-air market and the one "King Super" in huge hunks. The butcher would cut off a chunk wherever you pointed. If you knew where the good cuts were, you could do pretty well. It was all the same price. There was no such thing as a rare steak. Everything was cooked to death as the flies and other insects had free rein to light wherever they pleased. Even worse were the open-air markets. Nothing was fixed price so each purchase required time to bargain. The smell of urine was always present. Fruits and vegetable were often grown in night soil (human excrement). Meat was sometimes hard to identify. I remember seeing what looked too much like skinned human infants. The hawker said they were monkeys. Hmmm. Beggars were everywhere with diseases we couldn't even name. Food handlers were under no obligation to wash their hands or turn their faces away when they coughed.

We sometimes would send our cook or our small boy to the docks to meet ships to buy fresh fish or something we wanted that we couldn't find in the stores—like soy sauce.

The local mainstay diet was pounded yam. It was eaten with their fingers. Also popular was egusi soup. It was thickened with ground seeds and typically made from leafy vegetables, tomatoes, okra or chili peppers, fermented beans and beef, goat, fish or crayfish. A basic "everything but the kitchen sink" recipe.

For safety reasons, because it was expensive, and because there simply wasn't anything in the stores like pet food, Stateside brooms, or cosmetics, we bought in bulk through the Embassy. Every three months, families would take turns putting an order together. Phones worked well, probably due to the British presence, but there weren't very many of them so people would come by the house to place their order. Everything had to be purchased by the case. If you really didn't want a case of yellow cake mix or shampoo, you could work with another family or two and share the goods. These orders included toilet paper, Kleenex, soup, packaged rice, toothpaste, syrup, cleaning products, almost anything you would expect to see in a Stateside market. Can't remember which now, but the cases of meat came from one country and everything else from another. When the cases came in, the Embassy sent out a notice to the employees. That set off two or three days of a steady stream of people at your door. Or if you had to pick up your goods somewhere, to load it in your car, unload it, and put it away.

The "putting it away" got tricky. We were fortunate to have floor to ceiling shelves in a room off the kitchen. We set up an inventory system to keep track. Since the household help could not read, we put a card under each group of items with the total number of goods marked at the top. When an item was taken from the shelf, the card was marked with the old four slashes and a cross bar method. When the slashes got close to the first number, it was time to order more.

There was a tiny room at the Embassy that they jokingly called the commissary. We could buy a few things like shaving cream, cigarettes, some liquor or a case of butter. Try adding a family of seven's leftovers to a case of butter in a fourteen cubic-foot refrigerator sometime.

> **Note:** The freezer had to accommodate four plastic canteens every night as well. The water at the school was not potable and the kids took frozen water with them every morning.

Begging was a national sport, especially in Nigeria. People with huge goiter lumps, missing limbs, and every kind of crippling injury would jerk grocery bags out of your hands to load them in your car and expect a tip. Often large numbers of people would crowd around you to the point where you literally would be forced back against the building or your car. They all wanted money or to sell you something. It was frightening at times. I know the kids were afraid of some of the crippled people. They would push against you and wave their disability in your face. Some were pretty awful.

BLACK MAGIC AGAIN

It was a surprise to find black magic in the Philippines. It was not a surprise to find it in Nigeria. This time it was juju. It was so prevalent that it had its own marketplace.

On our first day in Lagos, we were warned by the Embassy to watch for bodies in driveways at night. Why? The typical house or apartment building in Lagos was behind a wall or fence. Most streets had open sewers. They were a cement ditch that ran parallel to the street between the wall and the pavement. The driveway ran over the sewer, through the gate, and to the house.

Night watchmen, called Watch Nights, would lie down across the driveway just behind the gate and go to sleep. If anyone drove into the driveway, he would wake up and open the gate. If the wall had no gate, it became a serious problem as the guards wore dark clothing and had dark skin. It would be very easy to run over them.

One might ask: If these men were guarding your house, why were they asleep? There was a simple answer. Our Watch Night, Obadiah, showed me the three jujus he bought at the local open-air juju market. He was proud to tell me that they were superior because he paid a hefty sum for them. It was hard to imagine any power in the popsicle sticks with string wrapped around and around in intricate high and low patterns. In any case, we were safe from harm because one was placed at the back of the house and another was placed on each side. Obidiah watched the front—when he was awake. It was comforting to know that were being so closely guarded.

I suppose I should add here that even though we found it hard to believe the jujus would keep the house safe, the Nigerians didn't. A guard asleep in the driveway meant jujus were nearby. So, in an odd way, they worked.

STRANDED AT TARKWA BAY

We lived on an island, but there was no recreational beach. For a "day at the beach" you had to catch a banana boat and travel six kilometers across Tarkwa Bay. These boats ran on a Nigerian schedule. That meant they started sometime in the morning and when the last boat left the beach for the mainland—you'd better be on it. The banana boat looked like an overgrown rowboat with an awning roof. It held about 40 people on rough, board seats. They traveled from pier to pier. You had to climb straight up or down a wooden ladder from the pier to the boat. Kinda scary with little kids, as the boat bounced around in the waves.

The destination was a beautiful, pristine beach with pure white sand against a green three-canopy jungle. The area was wild and isolated. Coconuts lay in the sand under the trees that dotted the beach. Locals would shimmy up the tall trunks and shake them for a few shilling. The coconuts were yours to eat, if you could figure out how to break them open.

Small, round, screened huts about six feet tall were for rent by the day. Young men were also for hire to guard your hut. Until we got to know some of the "regulars," you never knew exactly how safe your belongings were.

> **Janice's comments:** I absolutely loved it there except for my "shark" bite. I was floating way out on an inner tube when a jellyfish wrapped its tentacle around my ankle. I couldn't feel my foot anymore. I think it was numb from the sting. I started yelling, "shark" because I thought my foot was gone. Dad freaked out and got me out of the water, pulled my foot up and then got really mad at me for yelling shark and scaring the wits out of everyone on the beach who had scrambled for safety.

One day, waiting for the last boat, people were pushing and shoving to be first in line. A British woman was rude and over-anxious and nearly knocked Jim over the edge of the pier. He could have drowned or been crushed between the pier and the boat. Al grabbed him in time. He made some comment to the woman. Her husband stepped in and things quieted down. Instead of an apology, she made the comment that Jim was in her way. Colonial British could be really nasty.

We found our dog, Charlie, at Tarkwa. He was skinny and scruffy with a tail that made a right turn. Someone had slammed it in a screen door. We gave in to the kid's begging and took him home. After way too many trips to the Vet, he looked pretty good when his fur coat fell out and grew back in another color. Poor Charlie was hit by a mammy wagon (bus) in front of our house, but he survived. Incidentally, the only wild animal I saw in Nigeria was a monkey at the Vet's office.

> **Note:** Due to the war, the Embassy would not give me permission to leave Lagos so we didn't travel to the bush country. Al traveled north to the Muslim city of Kano on occasion. It is the second largest city.

We went to the beach with our neighbors from the German Embassy. After they arrived home, one of her daughters couldn't find her eye glasses. Her mother and I decided to go back to the beach the next day to see if we could find them. Evidently, no one went to Tarkwa on a weekday. We were alone on the pier. We had to bargain and pay an exorbitant price to get the driver to take out the boat just for us. The second our feet touched the pier, the driver turned the boat around and left saying he would come back in two hours. An eerie feeling crept over us. There was nothing on the beach except empty huts, sand and the jungle. It was only accessible by boat. No one was around for miles. And this was Africa.

A quick search produced the missing glasses. We watched for the boat. It didn't come. There was no way to call anyone. A phone probably wouldn't have worked anyway. We waited two hours, then three, then four; then finally accepted the fact that the boat may not be coming back.

Near the equator, daylight is from six in the morning to six at night all year long. It was going to get dark soon and the bay was dangerous at night. It was time to start planning to spend the night. The pile of coconuts was easy to collect. A rock to break them open was another matter.

The sun was beginning to lower into the ocean when we heard the motor. The boat driver had enjoyed some ginger beer, taken a nap, and forgotten us.

NOW YOU SEE THEM, THEN YOU DON'T

Citizenship can be lost if you stay out of the US too long, so we were on our way back home. We found housing for Bassie, his family, and Sunday. Justine went back to her family. We were at the Lagos airport. Once the twenty suitcases and a big trunk were checked through Customs, we took a collective deep breath and sat down in the restaurant to wait for our plane.

The Embassy could only give us fifty US dollars. The rest of our currency was in pounds and shillings, except for a pile of change we accumulated at the airport that was from other African countries. We wanted to save some of the coins for our collection so we picked those out of the pile, then dumped the rest on the table so we could see how much we actually had to spend. After figuring out the conversions from all the various currencies into the equivalent Nigerian pounds and shillings, we had about enough to pay for the meal, a few pounds, and the fifty dollars in cash. It had to last until we arrived in New York.

From the restaurant, you could see the area where luggage was loaded onto carts. Butch was watching all the activity and saw our suitcases being loaded—not onto an airport cart—but onto a private pickup truck. Someone was stealing our suitcases! Al and Butch ran back through the airport, grabbed two security officers, and stopped the theft. We all watched as they unloaded the suitcases from the truck and onto the airport carts. Thank Heaven Butch was paying attention.

Al was told just two days before we left Lagos that our cruise to New York was not going to happen. The State Department had issued a new rule that no one would be traveling by ship anymore. We would be flying to New York via Morocco instead. He was also told that his request for transfer back to the States was granted and was effective that day. We had packed for a vacation, not a permanent move. We had to scurry to pack everything else we owned. Usually, there was time to find a new assignment before the transfer. Not knowing how long it would take to find a new assignment, we were afraid to spend a lot of money staying in Morocco, or anywhere else, before going home. It seemed like something always prevented us from taking advantage of our layovers. We managed to miss Tel Aviv, Athens, Nairobi, and now Rabat.

We spent a few hours at the airport in Rabat, then boarded a plane for New York. Not very long into the trip, we learned that all but one of the flight attendants had eaten something in Rabat and were seriously ill with food poisoning. Several women volunteered to help serve the meals—so did Butch, Jim, and Janice. The kids had a wonderful time following instructions from the one attendant that was well. They helped her a lot. I was proud of them and they were a big hit with the passengers.

We arrived in New York late at night and new troubles arose. Our trunk was missing. We spent two hours running from one office to another and filling out forms. It finally appeared. We had to board another plane for Washington DC at six in the morning. The kids were so tired they were falling down. To our surprise, nothing was open at the airport.

We called several hotels near the airport and found a small room with two twin beds. The older kids took the beds, we made a pad of blankets for Eric on the floor, and Al and I slept in flimsy chairs. To make matters worse, after living in countries for so long where the power was off nearly as often as it was on—the electricity went off while I was in the shower. What a big disappointment. That wasn't supposed to happen in the United States of America.

At 4:30 a.m., we headed again for the airport. We were all starving. Guess what—the restaurants were still not open, and we still couldn't get any American currency. On the plane we ate the peanuts like they were our last meal. My brother met us in DC and immediately took us to breakfast. What a trip!

Our Lagos House

Open Sewers

Open Air Market

Head-ties

WASHINGTON DC

April 1971 to June 1973

It was good to be back in the United States for awhile.

WHAT DADDY DID AT HIS DC OFFICE

A Program Officer was needed in Washington DC to charter food shipments to Bangladesh for the Food for Peace Program. Al applied for the job.

The starvation in Bangladesh made headlines for months. Food for Peace was a Title II program managed by USAID. It works with US voluntary organizations and international organizations such as the Red Cross, UNICEF (United Nations Emergency Children's Fund), and the World Food Program. Countries all over the world were donating food. Al had to find a way to have it picked up and delivered or, if the country volunteered its own ship, schedule the docking and unloading. Not every ship can enter every port. Maritime Law in international waters is complicated. Each country has its own little quirks regarding their own waters. The documents still used the flowery language of the fifteen hundreds. It was the good ship XYZ, sound and tight, and always afloat.

Al tells a story: He was trying to find out whether a particular port could accept a deep-water draft ship. His maps didn't give him the information. The Library of Congress couldn't help. Offices at the State Department didn't know. People kept telling him to call Al Stone—that Al knew all about these ports. He was being referred back to himself.

Note: It was a great opportunity to add to our stamp collection as he was contacting people all over the world—some were little teeny countries I had never heard of.

DC DOES ITS OWN THING

We spent two years in the States. People in DC talked a lot of the time about our government and those who were governing. Actually, the whole world was talking about our government because we were right in the middle of the Watergate scandal. Rumors were the main topic of conversation. On the good side, we loved being around those who were making history, and the endless hours of discussion and debate over events that were changing the path of our country. (Sadly, we find more and more apathy now.)

Attending American Schools overseas caused a problem when we returned to the States—especially for Butch. He had more than enough units to graduate, but needed required things like PE and Civics. He finished what he needed in summer school between his junior and senior year, then graduated the next June just days before his sixteenth birthday. All of our kids were way ahead of their classmates both academically and socially. Someone said the other kids in school "seemed like babies." Our kids were accustomed to Embassy protocol and large social functions.

We began to realize when we got back to the States that girls one to two years older than our boys were attracted to them. Janice, too, found the much older boys more interesting than boys her own age. We worried about what they were learning from these older kids! Poor Butch wasn't even old enough to drive to his senior prom. He had to double-date to keep Mom or Dad from driving him to the dance. The adjustment coming back was hard.

The house in Alexandria was nice, but the area wasn't. One of the kid's bikes was stolen and Jim was mugged by some teens. The schools weren't so great either. After the one-year lease expired, we found a house with a huge yard in Annandale on Rose Lane.

A fierce storm hit the day of our move. To expedite things, paintings were propped up against the basement walls. Boxes of books and things we didn't need to worry about right away were on the basement floor, to be moved upstairs later. The window wells for the basement windows were at ground level. Water filled the window wells overnight and poured down the walls. There was a foot-deep pool by the next morning. The insurance company said we should have checked the wells. There are few, if any, basements in California or in the tropics. It didn't occur to us.

The silk paintings were damaged the most. A metal box containing our marriage certificate, baptismal records and other important documents, was not water-proof. We lugged the books upstairs and placed them on the floor in every room. We flipped all the pages of all the books as they dried as often as we could. I hated to lose so many, but especially the one autographed by John Kennedy.

Living on the northeastern seaboard of the United States is a lot like living in a history book. We took every opportunity to visit sites like Harpers Ferry, Gettysburg, Valley Forge, the Liberty Bell, Amish country, Kitty Hawk, and Mount Vernon. In DC, we toured the White House, the Senate building, the Lincoln, Jefferson and Washington monuments, the National Mint, FBI headquarters, and the Smithsonian. We bought a fourteen-foot travel trailer and parked it at Bull Run. Butch and Jim rode their bikes there during the summer.

In our day you could spend a day at the White House on a Congressional tour. The title is misleading. Anyone could contact his congressman and request tickets for the special guided tour of the White House. It was both a good day and a bad day for our tour. Indira Gandhi, the Prime Minister of India, was visiting. Many of the rooms were in use and not open to the tour. A small stage was set up on the lawn and President Nixon and Ms. Gandhi treated us to a speech. Both came down into the crowd and shook hands.

> **Note:** As an American, I was embarrassed by the display. Believe it or not, men dressed as medieval herald trumpeters, complete with banners, were on each stair and played their horns as the two exited the White House to reach the lawn. President Nixon's chair plainly stated, "The President" on the back. His makeup was thick and did something weird to his facial wrinkles when he smiled.

Each year there is a Veteran's Day program at Arlington Cemetery. We wanted to visit President Kennedy's grave and see the moving ceremony at the Tomb of the Unknown Soldier. We decided to go on that day. For the occasion, a podium was set up for the formal program. Vice President Agnew was the keynote speaker.

During the summer, the Marines hold fantastic programs in front of the Marine Memorial. The statue itself is huge and impressive. The Marine Band plays and the special drill teams perform with incredible precision. They march without direction on grass. This prevents hearing the cadence as they perform. They don't miss a step.

Army Headquarters has a special Christmas program each year. The all male chorus sings Christmas and National songs. Tickets are limited, but Al was able to get some for us. It was a stirring performance that we will never forget.

We attended the black-tie State Department party for the Fourth of July. Al was involved in the planning that year. Most of the attendees were members of Congress. The rooms set aside for the party were on an upper floor. Windows were eye-level with the top of the Washington monument where the fireworks explode. We were practically on top of the display. Vice President and Mrs. Agnew made an appearance. They watched the fireworks with us and mingled with the crowd.

The sofas, chairs tables, and desks in the rooms were antiques from the White House. A past president had used each piece. The beautiful banquet table under the exquisite crystal chandelier was set with fine linens and tableware and large platters of the little, inexpensive McDonald's hamburgers with a pickle garnish. There were all those people in their tuxedos and formals sitting on those priceless antiques with hamburgers. We ate our meals standing up. We were afraid to sit down for fear we would spill something.

Al was invited to a ritzy Washington DC Art Society dinner. I went along. One of his projects while working in DC was to logistically support a university's efforts to unearth the wonderful temples in Guatemala called Tikal. They still didn't have the roads completed to access the site and were just discovering all that was there. The club was very interested. Al was to show slides and give a presentation.

Tuxedos and formal gowns were very much in order. The dinner, along with a display of miniature art, was in the James Monroe mansion. We were seated at the head table with the president of the Club. On my left was the head of the Security and Exchange Commission. He had just returned from a safari. On my right was an elderly woman who owned the fanciest hotel in DC. They knew each other and were engrossed in his story about the safari. When I leaned forward to take a bite, they leaned back and chatted. When I leaned back, they acted annoyed and leaned forward to chat some more. It became a comedy. Each bite was a challenge. As the person at the head of the table finishes each course, that course is cleared. If they have manners, they wait until everyone is finished. My food kept going back to the kitchen.

The main course was finally served. Most everyone was finished eating. I waited, but the president lingered and lingered before finishing her course. I couldn't stand it any longer. I had to call home to check on the kids. I knew dessert and coffee was being served upstairs on the antique china, so I decided to leave the table and call.

Etiquette says that you cannot rise from the table until the person at the head of the table rises, signaling the end of the meal. I got up anyway, turned around to push my chair back, and realized not a word was being said. Every face at the table was turned toward me with a look of disbelief. I couldn't have attracted more attention if I had thrown up all over the table. I just kept going and made my call. The high society etiquette on this evening translated into just plain bad manners.

Al was still trying to achieve his goal and found his way into the Latin America Bureau. He was appointed as head of the Central American Common Market Bank, but still working in DC. He was attending a conference in Guatemala when the opportunity to actually work in Latin America came. During the Christmas season of 1972, Managua, Nicaragua collapsed in a massive earthquake. Eighty per cent of the commercial buildings were leveled. The death toll was in the thousands. The United States negotiated a loan with Nicaragua to clear the rubble and rebuild the city. Al was assigned the job of administering that loan.

He was sent to Managua to survey the damage and begin the recovery. While he was gone, I made arrangements to move the family. He came back to escort us to our new home.

Jefferson Monument and Japanese gift of Cherry trees

FROM DC TO MANAGUA, NICARAGUA

May 1973

We pulled a travel trailer through detours in corn fields and took turns watching the road.

SOUTHWARD HO

The adventurer in Al was coming out once again and he wanted to drive. I was leery, but he thought of everything. It is probably something one should do once in their life, but once is enough. We headed toward the Carolinas in the hot summer of 1973 leaving Butch behind. He was attending classes at California Lutheran College in California and wanted to remain in the States over the summer.

Automobile warranties are void the minute you drive out of the United States. Hertz and Avis use Fords and Chevrolets and have agencies that honor their warranties all over the world. You might even get lucky and find a part for them overseas. Most Foreign Service families drive one or the other. We bought a Mercury station wagon from Hertz. To be prepared, we packed up extra parts and a wheel.

We knew that six hundred square blocks were gone in Managua and facilities were scarce. The fourteen-foot travel trailer went with us in case we had to live in it for some period of time. The manual said it slept six. We should have noticed that it did not say, "sleeps six comfortably."

We arrived in Greenville, North Carolina on a Sunday. The restaurants we passed were not open. A police officer in a traffic circle gave us directions. He was so polite, we decided to make a u-turn and go back by the circle to tell him how much we appreciated the courtesy. Guess we hadn't realized how rude people were in DC. He thanked us, then flagged down a family and asked them to lead us to a restaurant. After all these years, that kind gesture still comes up in conversation.

We drove through Georgia, Alabama, Mississippi, Louisiana, and crossed into Mexico at the Texas border. Don't tell anyone, but we stopped on the US side of the border and found a garage that would illegally take the smog equipment off the car. This gave us better mileage and a motor that ran more efficiently on Mexican gas at high altitudes.

I don't recall many things about the US side of the trip except for the dead cow in the road in Alabama and Al taking the older kids to tour the battleship Alabama. Mosquitoes in some places were so horrible that there would be spots of blood on the pillows in the morning in spite of all the sprays. We walked down Bourbon Street in New Orleans but couldn't go in most places with minors. The Alamo was a must visit in San Antonio. Somewhere on the highway, cars started to honk at us. Seconds later, a huge semi-truck passed us on the right shoulder at high speed. The Lord was guiding that truck inches from us, in the dirt.

Al was setting up the trailer in a Texas campground. It was hot and sticky so I took the kids to the pool. It was "T" shaped with the deep end at the top of the "T". I sat and read at the shallow end where Eric was playing. I swear I heard someone call, "Mom." I looked up. Eric was gone. He had been at the edge just seconds before. I could see him sinking to the bottom. There was no diving board and it was not posted that between the two three-foot shallow sides was a deep strip for divers. Eric had stepped off the underwater ledge into ten feet of water and had no doubt swallowed half the pool.

I screamed and jumped in. The kids got to him before I did. Janice dove under him, pushing him up to the surface with her head and shoulders with the other kids helping. With CPR he coughed up water and started to breathe. I am convinced he would have drowned except for her. I still cry and get upset when I think of it. That pool owner will never forget how angry Al was.

Once over the border, it became more dangerous to drive. It was the rainy season, so there were monsoon downpours nearly every day.

> **Note:** Rain tends to fall about the same time of day in the tropics, so you could almost predict the downpours.

There were no fences to prevent cattle and horses from wandering out on the roadway. Most of the trucks, and many of the cars, had big cattle guards installed on the front bumper just in case they met up with something on four legs. We didn't have a cattle guard, so we took turns watching the road for hazards.

Many people walked on the roads too. They made travel even more dangerous because they didn't always watch where they were going. Sadly, we saw obviously inebriated men staggering across the lanes, especially in the evening hours. That added to their disregard for our station wagon and trailer.

The first stop was Monterrey, Mexico. We found an almost new KOA campground with modern hook-ups. We arrived without incident, except that the lawn chairs we had tied to the back of the trailer had disappeared. Light-fingered little devils down there. We hired a guide and drove all over the city.

Our car barely ran due to Mexican gas and the high altitude, but it chugged along. Al kept teasing and telling us to pedal faster when we were climbing an especially steep hill. The next stop was Mexico City. The thin air and terrible smog from all the diesel vehicles made it hard to breathe. Jim was especially susceptible and felt sick the whole time we were there.

We did it again. We missed many of the tourist places we wanted to visit. They were not open. It was some sort of holiday.

You take your life in your own hands on their crowded subway. Keeping seven of us together was a challenge. Interesting, though. Ruins were found during construction, so they just left everything there and built the subway around them. More wonderful ruins were in Oaxaca and Mexico City. The Indians did amazing things with the buildings and the agriculture. Many of the crops were terraced over very steep hills. I don't know how they walked on them, much less planted crops.

Central American borders are open between the hours of 6:00 a.m. and 6:00 p.m. It was possible to wait in the seemingly endless line of cars only to have the gates close as you approached. Even with our Official passports, the Customs agents often spent well over an hour looking through our luggage, the car, and every drawer and shelf in the trailer. Actually, I think it was more curiosity than anything else. We found ourselves timing everything to the border crossings.

> **Note:** Even though a passport was not required in Mexico at the time, the State Department required us to make known our status by carrying our Official passports.

Travel during the rainy season created some unique problems. In Mexico City, we found out the hard way that when a manhole is under a couple feet of water in an intersection with no cover, the front tire of your car can roll into it and get stuck. Four or five Mexican men immediately jumped to our aid. With all of us in water up to our knees, and pushing the car and trailer back and forth, it somehow rolled free. No one would take a peso for their help.

We went from manholes to cornfields. Because the rain had washed out the main road, we found ourselves pulling a trailer through the middle of a water-logged cornfield. The forest of corn stalks towered over the car. At times we couldn't tell if we were headed out of the field or just wandering around. Except for some shattered nerves and some missing paint, we made it.

Guatemala is mountainous with small, unevenly paved roads and almost no road signs to guide you. As luck would have it, we met two soldiers at the border between Mexico and Guatemala. They were on leave, knew the way to Guatemala City, and needed a ride. It is a darned good thing we took them with us or we would still be in the hills looking for a way out.

At a roadblock not far from the border, Mexican soldiers flagged us down. They wanted to go through the luggage, car, and the trailer once again. Our hitch-hikers decided they didn't want to wait. Waving their guns around, they convinced the soldiers at the roadblock that they really didn't need to search us after all.

We drove higher and higher into the mountains. Places to eat and rest became almost non-existent. The road was narrow, windy, full of chunks of concrete, straight up on one side, and straight down on the other. We were starving and drove for miles without seeing anything except a fruit cart. We bought all the vendor's bananas and pineapples, pulled over as far as we could without sliding off the edge of the mountain, and had lunch.

Miles and miles and miles down that awful road, we stopped again, only to discover that our cat was nowhere to be found. To this day, I cannot imagine how it got out. We were sure we put her back in the trailer at the previous stop. Janice was devastated and mad at us the rest of the trip for not going back to try to find it. I still feel awful about that poor thing, but a round trip up that road to try to find a cat which could have been anywhere didn't make sense. We couldn't seem to hang onto cats.

Then it started to rain. Have you ever been in monsoon rain? It was nearly impossible to see, much less travel. Everyone got very quiet.

We needed a break from the rain and the crowding in the trailer, so we rented rooms at a beautiful hotel when we arrived in Guatemala City. It was raining so hard that we got drenched just running the few feet from the trailer door to the hotel canopy. Poor Al made too sharp a turn in the parking lot and a safety feature let the trailer hitch give way. He had to get into that downpour and re-assemble it just to park.

Al had been to Guatemala City on an earlier trip. He knew of a good restaurant across the street. We went and let the kids order whatever they wanted from room service. When we returned, we found trays of an odd assortment of food. Room service had been closed, so Jim called the Manager who took them downstairs to ransack the leftovers in the hotel refrigerator. We were proud of him for being so resourceful.

The city of San Salvador sits at the base of a huge volcano which occasionally erupts. The hotel was brand new with almost no customers. It was subsidized by the government to try to increase tourist trade. Since we shared the hotel employees with only a handful of guests, service was spectacular.

We walked downtown to have dinner. Just outside the restaurant, two cars bumped into each other. The drivers got out and yelled and waved their arms, then decided it was just too hot to argue in the street. They left the two cars in the middle of the street and moved the argument inside where it was air-conditioned. They each ordered a drink and kept on yelling and waving. That says a lot about life in Central America.

On the way to the Honduran border, traffic slowed to a crawl, then stopped. A farmer had two enormous Brahma bulls in a flatbed, short-sided trailer that had tipped over. The bulls were confused and maybe even hurt. They were charging at people on the road who had stopped to help. Our trailer attracted one of the bulls. He charged. Seeing a giant Brahma bull grow larger and larger as it gets closer and closer from a head-on perspective is terrifying. Al somehow got out of his way. I don't know how he did it without running over something or somebody.

Jim was starting to run a fever and didn't feel well. We were getting worried, but only had one more border to cross to get to Managua. In late afternoon, we stopped in San Miguel, a tiny town on the border, and planned to cross at 6:00 a.m. The motel had so many roaches that we rented a room, but planned to sleep in the trailer. I wasn't feeling too well either, so I laid down for a nap and asked Al to watch the kids. A dental student was on his way to Nicaragua to work free of charge in a clinic for the summer. His car was on the fritz. Al was helping him.

The motel had just cleaned their pool and was refilling it with water. This made a water slide effect over the tiles. The kids were slipping down the water slide when Janice had her hands forced out from under her. Her face came down on the pool tiles and half of each of her front teeth were broken off. There was no dental office anywhere near San Miguel. Thank God for the dental student. He and Al took her to a farmacia (pharmacy). No prescription was needed to buy codeine and some sort of cream that we put on gauze to help ease the pain and block air from passing by her teeth.

We straggled into the Intercontinental Hotel in Managua with Jim now running a fever of one hundred three degrees. I was never so glad to get anywhere. The Embassy made arrangements for Al to take Janice to a German dentist, and the hotel sent a doctor who didn't speak a word of English to the room for Jim. They didn't teach me any medical terms in Spanish class. We were off to a rocky start in Latin America.

MANAGUA, NICARAGUA

June 1973 to July 1976

It would be difficult to tell the difference between a photo of a bombed-out European city during World War II and a photo of Managua after the quake.

WHAT DADDY DID AT HIS NICARAGUENSE OFFICE

The document to manage the loan of one hundred and forty million dollars to rebuild Managua was hundreds of pages. Much of the money was to be spent purchasing goods and services from the United States. Al worked with counterparts in the Nicaraguense and British government. Nicaragua added matching funds of one hundred and forty million cordobas. The British Embassy donated or purchased the majority of the beds and equipment when the hospitals were completed. Before the British monies were expended, Al was appointed by the British government to manage the remaining funds.

How do you rebuild an entire city where there are hundreds of blocks of tangled and twisted masonry and metal? Al did a superb job. Congress voted his project in Managua the most successful USAID project for each of the three years we were there.

Six hundred square blocks and over eighty per cent of the commercial buildings were gone. Six thousand died. Twenty thousand were injured. Two hundred and fifty thousand were left homeless. Most of the damage was in the downtown area where high-rises collapsed. The walls of tilt-up buildings fell to the outside and the roofs came crashing down, not allowing time for the occupants to get out alive.

The smell of the fire that spread throughout the city lingered in the air. Water was still gushing here and there through the wreckage from broken water mains weeks after the quake. Barbed wire was thrown up everywhere. It took months to find all the bodies—if they ever did. Sadly, some probably became part of the rubble. Initially, there was no water or electricity. Managua was a massive pile of rubble. Most street lighting was gone so the city was pitch black at night. It was made more eerie because the December 23rd quake had scrambled brightly colored Christmas decorations into the debris. Sadly, many vendors from the countryside come into the city at that time of year to sell their goods on the sidewalks. No one will ever know the real death toll on that awful day.

The US Embassy collapsed. A breezeway between the two buildings acted like a battering ram and knocked down both buildings. A secretary was killed. Embassy personnel temporarily moved into the dust and heat in tents on the Ambassador's Residence lawn. There were stories in Washington papers about our Ambassador's wife. The Pulitzer Prize-winning journalist, Jack Anderson, called her the "Ugly American." She turned the filter off in the pool so that no one could jump in and cool off. The Residence bathrooms were closed. The Embassy employees eventually opened offices in temporary quarters. By the time we got our family settled in, Al had a decent place to work.

Al's first project was to clear the rubble. Over three thousand men were hired. They were fed three meals a day. Their families were housed in a hurriedly-built temporary settlement. Most of the rubble was cleared either by hand or with simple tools. The rubble was dumped into Lake Managua, creating a causeway. There were backhoes, but not nearly enough. It sounds terrible to say that was good, but it had the side effect of giving these men work with pay at a time when their jobs were gone, because all the buildings were gone. Many came in from the provinces to find work in the reconstruction. The city was quickly swollen to several times its original size.

> **Note:** Until water could be restored, it was brought into the barrios in barrels. Several hundred people either became ill or died because no one could read the English word "Insecticide" on some of the barrels.

Traffic was a horrible problem. First, few streets were passable. Second, if a street was cleared and open, the traffic lights or signs were gone. Imagine what it would be like driving in a large city with no traffic signs or signals. Not sure how, but the crews actually left a telephone pole in the dead center of one road. The projects on Al's "To Do" list all had the same high priority.

As rubble was cleared, streets were opened. Schools and buildings that survived the quake were reinforced and open again to the public. Homes and commercial buildings began to appear. There was a lot of discussion regarding building codes and strict standards were enforced. The extraordinary result of this dreadful disaster was a brand new city with much safer structures.

The National Cathedral was severely damaged and was scheduled for demolition. A cry went up to save it. Al found someone who developed a hot epoxy that held everything together and the Cathedral was rebuilt. It made newspaper headlines.

The hospitals were gone, along with most of the equipment and ambulances, except for Velez Paiz, a badly damaged deserted hospital. The government military hospital was destroyed so those patients were moved to what was left of Velez Paiz. Beds were crammed together. Bodies were on the floor. Dogs ran through the halls. Few windows had screens. There was no working kitchen. The "laundry" was a boiling pot over an open fire and clotheslines. Electricity wasn't dependable so the minimal equipment wasn't either. After three babies died, they realized the home-style box freezer they were using to store formula was set at too high a temperature.

Al not only whipped that hospital into shape overnight, he added a wing with one hundred fifteen new beds. To accommodate the immediate need, sixty-six clinics were quickly manned and equipped around the city. The military put up two tent field hospitals.

It typically takes one to two years just to complete the drawings for a new hospital. Al had the drawings, the buildings, and the equipment in two new, fully functional hospitals in just over two years. He had the Nicaraguense men working overtime and weekends—something unheard of. He made a trip to Miami with seven million dollars and purchased beds, equipment, and supplies. It was phenomenal.

While Al was in Miami, the workers were supposed to install lead in the cement walls before finishing the x-ray room. Well, someone forgot. Rather than hold up the grand opening, the lead was attached to the room walls with glue or something creative. It didn't look so great, but it worked.

We had a huge party of about one hundred people at our house to celebrate the opening of the hospitals. Even Ambassador and Mrs. Shelton appeared. Most of the Nicaraguense ministers of government were there. Sir James Duncan, the ambassador from Great Britain and his First Secretary attended. We sent a driver to pick up some Mariachi bands and had three bands rotating all night. Three of the employees from the Embassy were hired as bartenders. They set up a huge bar on the ping pong table.

My Mother was visiting at the time. It was near her birthday so we had everybody sing Las Mañanitas in Spanish and Happy Birthday to her. She was pretty impressed with the crowd, except for one of the ministers, who got a little too inebriated and took a nap under the dining room table. She and Sir James hit it off and they danced and chatted throughout the evening.

Al was elected and then re-elected President of the Foreign Service Association. He acted as liaison between the members and liaison between the membership and the Ambassador. One interesting aspect of the job is that he was the single person in the Embassy that could send an Official telegram under his own name without the Ambassador's approval. It was set up that way so that the Association could file a grievance with the State Department without the Ambassador's knowledge. Every other telegram was sent under the Ambassador's name.

This didn't have much to do directly with the rebuilding of Managua, but there was a tremendous need for a road that led to the city from the coffee producing farms. Al set about completing a two hundred sixty kilometer road so the campesinos could get their produce to market. The farmers were thrilled to cut down the travel time—or in some cases—able to reach these markets for the first time. Truly a win/win situation.

A NEW WAY OF LIFE

Our house was rented from an Argentine couple. The four bedroom house was a wonderful surprise. It had three living rooms, three baths, and five small patios. It was just around the corner from the Embassy and only four and a half kilometers from the center of town. As most of the furniture in their warehouse had been destroyed, the Embassy couldn't provide furnishings for one of the living rooms and the dining room. Al went out and bought a saw, some wood, and some leather. He made great-looking tables, chairs, a settee, book shelves, and even a barbecue pit.

Our landlady's Argentine Spanish had the beautiful soft "th" sound, but with my high school Spanish, I could barely understand her. I was finally able to grasp that her maid would remain in the house to help us. The maid was an older woman who, it turns out, had no patience with a *gringa* who was struggling with Spanish—and she spoke no English. She put up with me less than two weeks. Then she left.

Many Americans hired Bluefields girls. These women were not Latin, but were descendants of African slaves. Bluefields, on the Atlantic Miskito Coast, was named for the Miskito Indians. At the time, it was only accessible by plane or boat on the nearly impassable Punta Gorda River. It was a steamy lagoon town that was once a British plantation colony with a slave economy. Bluefields girls were supposedly more desirable because they spoke English.

I looked for a "local" girl. The local girl I hired was actually from Lebanon. She was extremely shy and modest. The uniforms we bought her were just below the knee in length. She surprised me one morning with a similar fabric, hand-stitched to the hem, to make them calf length. Looked a little odd, I must say.

Even with Spanish classes, I continued to have learning problems. I remember the new maid trying to tell me we needed to buy peen-ee-sole, tee-day, and cah-my. I had her write it down. It was Pinesol, Tide, and Camay soap. I guess we were too much for her too because she didn't last very long either.

Note: Eric and I learned a lot of Spanish watching the Spanish version of Sesame Street on television.

Petronila (Neela) was about 18 years old. We got along great. She really enjoyed being with the kids. Unfortunately, she got pregnant out of wedlock and we had to let her go. I always felt a little guilty about that, but remember you are responsible for your employee's health issues. She had a normal pregnancy and we could have afforded the medical care. However, there is always the chance that you could get involved in a medical nightmare.

Neela came by to visit often, bringing the baby. Eric and I drove her home one day. She lived in a barrio that had fairly decent homes (by Nicaraguense standards). Some construction was opposite her house. I noticed a sort of berm about 18 inches high on one side of the very long narrow, dirt driveway. She was the end house so I made a "two or three try" turn around up against the berm and headed out of the barrio. I could then see, to my horror, that the berm was the edge of a huge crater about 50 feet deep and 20 feet wide. What its purpose was, I have no idea. I will always wonder how close to the edge of that thing I came when juggling the car back and forth.

We had several women work for us in the three years—always two at a time. All of the women did a great job, and were generally happy. Some of the superstitions were weird. God forbid you needed something ironed on a day during the lavendera's menstrual cycle. They believed that they would get sick if they ironed on one of those days. They wouldn't iron if their hair was wet either.

Our street was like many others now, having businesses located in homes. There was a Bank of America on the corner, an insurance agency next door and a Dr. Scholl's down the street. A hardware store was built a little later. Each of the businesses had a guard at night. We didn't seem to need one, as Kenny became great friends with all of them. As a result, they all looked out for us. He learned a lot of (probably good and bad) Spanish from those guards. Heaven only knows what else. He tells me that I don't want to know.

Felipe was our gardener and handyman almost from day one. His wife worked for us the last year we were there. They became our good friends. He allowed us to call him Felipe for all those years, even though his name was Felix. Even his wife called him Don Felipe. I got his name wrong during his first interview and he didn't want to embarrass me.

When his wife worked for us, he used our house as a stopover. It was nice for them and it was nice for us. On occasion, he would spend the night. They would sometimes sit and watch TV with us.

For some time after the quake, there was only enough water for use in the home. No one had any landscaping for that reason. When we finally could water the yard, Felipe turned our five patios into wonderful gardens with no money from us at all. He took pieces of this plant and pieces of that plant from our house and other customers. We all had beautiful yards. Of course, you could put a hoe handle in that rich soil and I swear, it would grow. Fertilizer was dirt from the field across the street so we didn't have to buy anything like that either.

Our household shipment arrived in what they called "lift vans." They were huge wooden boxes six feet square. Al got the idea of using the wood to build Felipe a house in his housing area called Open Three. Al asked an architect that worked with the Nicarguense government on the city reconstruction project to draw up some plans for a little one-bedroom house. While waiting for the drawings, we began taking the nine billion nails out of the three lift vans. There were an amazing number of boards when we were through. Everyone pitched in. Sometimes the kids complained a little, but kept going.

On weekends, Al and the kids built the house. It was one of the few with no dirt floor. Felipe had two children of his own. His brother was killed in the earthquake so he also had the brother's wife and two children living with him. I think there was an aunt or uncle as well.

It was hard to say good-bye when we left Managua. We gave Felipe everything that we didn't pack, including a TV set and some appliances. They had no electricity, but they could sell those things for extra money. We heard later that Open Two, Three, and Four had been leveled by the Sandinistas. We tried to contact Felipe through the Embassy, but we never heard. I hope that he and his family weren't hurt, but I am afraid they were right in the middle of it all.

GROCERY SHOPPING 107-110

We had fairly nice, modern markets as well as the local open air markets. Road side stands were very common. We also had a small commissary at the Embassy. Food was available in the markets, but very expensive. A can of Spam was four dollars or more. Beef was from Brahmas and was like shoe leather. I got pretty good at using marinades to tenderize. Poultry was not very good in any tropical country. Chickens and heat were a bad mix. Rice and beans was the mainstay for the Nationals. We learned to like some of the treats, like plantain fried in honey and butter. Yum.

I bought most of our food at the Supers. Their rice was in huge baskets on the floor. The vegetables were not good. (I remember coming back to the States, walking into a super-market, and seeing the beautiful vegetables and actually welling up with tears.) The meat department looked much like in the States. Eggs were displayed loose. I learned to bring a box to carry them home.

Food, blankets, and medical supplies were sent to Nicaragua after the quake by the United States and many other countries.

These gifts were supposed to be distributed without charge to local residents in need. We often found items on store shelves for sale that were plainly marked, "Gift of the United States of America. Not to be sold or exchanged." That was true in Vietnam and Nigeria as well. There were rumors that warehouses existed on the east coast of Nicaragua that were full of these gifts.

PROTOCOL AND ETIQUETTE

Ambassador Shelton's wife was the daughter of Cecil B. DeMille, the movie director. The wife of the Chief of Mission came with her car and driver to pick me up for the call to Mrs. Shelton. She was made comfortable in the living room. It was time to go, but I couldn't find my white gloves. She became distressed and insisted on loaning me one of hers. We were ready now, so I left her alone to tell the maid we were leaving. Unfortunately, our beagle, Elwood, was in the house. I heard a muffled cry and ran to the living room. I couldn't believe my eyes. There was the very stiff and formal wife of my husband's boss with her hat, fancy dress, and one glove, sitting on the edge of the sofa, and there was Elwood—happily humping her properly crossed leg! She avoided me at every Embassy function after that memorable introduction.

Some protocol requirements were circumvented. When the Ambassador is at an official Embassy function, Embassy personnel cannot leave that function until the Ambassador has vacated the premises. This made it awkward if the Ambassador was having a good time and wanted to stay until all hours. The solution was to have the Ambassador "officially" leave the function and then return informally, so people could go home.

Anastasio Somoza, the President of Nicaragua, was a graduate of West Point and preferred to speak English. We were invited to his Residence for a pool party. Al had gone on ahead. I was to meet him there.

The Embassy issued special identification cards to personnel, but mine wasn't ready yet. When I got to the Residence, there was a guard booth and a very imposing armed guard who wanted to see my Embassy identification. I don't know what possessed me, but I still had my Safeway grocery check-cashing card in my wallet with the great big red "S" on it. I pulled it out and waved it at him. He saw the "S" and thinking it stood for Somoza, let me pass. It is a wonder I wasn't shot for trying to sneak in. Al was not happy with me and neither was Ambassador Shelton.

Sir James Duncan, the ambassador from Great Britain, was a war hero. He had a wonderful, thick, Scottish accent. He was not married and I sometimes helped him at Official functions. The British Embassy has a dinner each year to honor the Queen on her birthday. It is a very formal, black-tie affair. The table is set with special china reserved for this special occasion. A setting for the Queen was placed at the head of the table. Before dinner was served, everyone stood and raised their glass wishing her a Happy Birthday. The man standing next to me added, "God love 'er."

Ambassador Shelton was a true southern gentleman and did something that I thought showed a lot of class. We were having dinner on the enclosed porch at the Residence one evening. After a wonderful meal, finger bowls with floating bougainvillea blossoms were brought to the table. There was a woman there who was at her first Post and not familiar with finger bowls. She picked up her spoon and dipped it into the finger bowl, picking up the blossom. She then put it into her mouth and ate it.

Ambassador Shelton saw what she did and picked up his spoon, dipped it into his finger bowl and ate his blossom, so she wouldn't be embarrassed. You know what is coming next.

We all picked up our spoons, dipped them into our fingerbowls and ate our bougainvillea blossoms too. Incidentally, I don't recommend bougainvillea blossoms in your regular diet. They taste awful.

Mrs. Shelton was another matter. The women at diplomatic missions were not allowed to work in-country. The reasoning was that she would take a job away from a National. Instead, we found ways to benefit charities or correct situations where help was needed. We held meetings to decide which projects to work on. Mrs. Shelton had a passion for bazaars to raise money. Somehow we always ended up with at least one bazaar a year which forced us to hand-make things to sell. Not a very popular idea. I was assigned—yes, I said assigned—the job one year of hemming a tablecloth and twelve napkins. I can't make square corners on a sewing machine much less by hand so I paid a tailor to do it. Mrs. Shelton didn't like them. She had them done over and put me on her "bad" list. The next year, we were selling home-baked pies. Notice the home-baked. They were store bought and baked at home.

LANGUAGE AND CULTURE

Cash was still king in Managua. An example is Jim's request to stay overnight with a friend at his dad's ranch. We knew the boy so we let him go. We nearly had a heart attack when we learned that the two boys and a driver had escorted a huge cash payroll to the ranch. Two teenagers rode shotgun over a enormous amount of money!

The Nicaraguense are a warmhearted people. They touch to show their affection. The embrazo (hug) is the typical greeting. My family became addicted and we all do a lot of embrazo-ing now. Al had a counterpart to his position within the Nicaraguense government. For some reason, he acted as though he resented

Al. He was stand-offish and would speak only Spanish. We knew he could speak English. It took many months for us to finally win him over. I knew I had won his approval when he gave me a lingering embrazo, held my hands in his, looked into my eyes and said in English, "Nancy, you are a big woman." I didn't understand all that he was trying to say, but I have no doubt that I will ever receive praise as genuine as that again.

In Nicaragua, as in most Latin American countries, the man is not master of his castle. His wife is. Within the walls of the home, the wife rules. Beyond the front door, she is respected and loved on a pedestal, but she is expected to stay on her perch. A beautiful custom showing respect is between a son and his mother. A son who enters the home is expected to find his mother and kiss her hand before he does anything else.

The kids picked up Spanish very quickly and are still fluent today. Al had a very large vocabulary. I could say much more than I could understand.

The Nicaraguense use a lot of slang and tend to cut off the last syllable or the last "s" of each word leaving the words not sounding anything at all the way they are spelled. Buenas Dias becomes "Buen Dia." Good luck understanding when they are spitting Spanish at you a mile a minute.

In the home, Al was called Señor and I was Doña Nancy. They have some interesting expressions like "Tengo un clavo." (I have a nail.) They mean they have a serious problem. The nail refers to the nail driven into the hand of Christ. I found one really useful slang word. Chunche means stuff. Do you know how many things you can call a chunche when you don't know the word in Spanish? We even named the cat Chunche.

Not having a good grasp on the language can cause some awkward moments. Attending parties I would often find myself sitting in a group and suddenly realize that everyone was looking directly at me, expecting me to respond to some comment or question. I would have absolutely no idea what to say. I found myself going to the bathroom, leaning up against the sink and just taking a deep breath—then going "once more into the fray." After the fourth or fifth trip down the hall, they must have wondered what was wrong with my bladder.

We had five small patios. Floor to ceiling paneled doors lined the entire length of the main living room that opened to one them. This was where most guests went outside when we had parties. Felipe wanted to plant some rather tall plants along the edge of the flagstone where the grass began. In my Spanish, I thought I told him not to plant them there because they were too tall for the guests to walk past and onto the grass. He told me later that I told him that I didn't want the plants there because they were too tall for the guests to pee over. He wondered what kind of parties we gave.

In Nicaragua, houses did not have numbers and streets did not have names. There were districts, so I guess that narrowed it down a bit. Things were either "toward or away from the lake" or "toward or away from the mountains." Our address was kilometro quatro y media, Carretera Sur, a la esquina BMW, 200 varas al lago. That translates to "kilometer four and a half, South Highway, the BMW dealership on the corner, 200 varas (about thirty-three inches) toward the lake." It always amazed me that anyone found us. In the first place, there was a house on both sides of the street. How did they know which one was ours? It helped a little when we got the horse, Chicharon (pork chitlins). I could tell them it was the house with the horse in the driveway.

When we first arrived in Managua, it was so hard to locate anything. Landmarks are used to give directions. Many of them have proper noun names. To locate something, you would be told to go to the landmark and then so many blocks toward the mountains, or so many blocks toward the lake.

For example, there was a monstrous tree called "Los Arbolitos" that was a commonly used marker. It took us awhile to figure it out, but the tree had been removed years before. As a newcomer, we didn't know that it didn't exist anymore. We spent a lot of time driving around looking for that darned tree.

After the earthquake, it was even worse. Many of the landmarks were gone. I wonder if they ever tried to fix the problem or if they just let people wander around looking for things. My guess is the latter.

THE AMERICAN SCHOOL

From Janice and Jim: The school was chicken coop-like-buildings. We had no air-conditioning, just ceiling fans. Rain was noisy on the corrugated metal roof. The dirt on our desks in the dry season was sometimes thick enough to write your name in. The chicken coops were temporary buildings put up by the Peace Corps. Some of our teachers were from the Peace Corps too. They came after the earthquake because the school had fallen down and some of the classes had to be held in tents. The fallen buildings still lay in rubble in the back. We used to go back there sometimes. Probably not too safe.

We had to go to school in shifts. The elementary school went in the morning and the junior high and high school went in the afternoon. We had a late start because there were not enough classrooms for all the grades. There was no cafeteria. There was a refreshment stand which was only a shack. Two ladies sold cokes, Tu Yo's (popsicles) and quesillos (tortillas with sun-cured onions and cheese). That was all we had to choose from except for the green mangoes on the trees that we used to climb. We got salt from the ladies at the stand. The acid burned your mouth. The elementary kids ate when they got home and we ate before we left for school.

I don't remember having PE (Physical Education) until we got to Nicaragua. They hired a woman to teach PE, but she was very fat. It was always too hot to do anything outside, so we just sat in the teacher's lounge and talked. There was one teacher who made us play a game that was a weird combination of soccer and basketball. I have never seen it since. The school did have bingo nights, dances and activities of that kind. Janice was crowned Princess on one occasion.

I don't know how good an education we received when sometimes we learned Algebra in Spanish. We learned most of our Spanish from the maids. We also loved the fact that all of our brothers and sisters went to one school. It was nice to know they were there even though we rarely saw them during the day.

There was an unstated rule among the kids in school. If someone new joined the school, which happened frequently, the rule was that you got to know everyone quickly because you were there only for a short time.

There was a big difference between the overseas schools and those in the US. It made it really awkward and we hated living in the States at first. It was harder to move to the US than any other country we had been in.

Jim said, "I had to write an essay on home during my freshman year in college. My professor was intrigued when I wrote that my home was where my family was, instead of a specific location as most of the other kids described. I still can't believe how well we have it in the States compared to other countries and how most Americans just have no idea and expect more.

For some reason, we decided to take turns with a neighbor to drive the kids to and from school. It wasn't until we had been doing this for some time that one of the kids told me they didn't want to rideshare anymore because she would make the sign of the cross before she left the driveway each morning. They were afraid. That would have made me nervous too. We stopped the ridesharing.

NOT YOUR USUAL MINISTRY MEETING

I was coming home from Spanish class one morning and walked in the front door to find Al and most of the Ministry of the Nicaraguense government in my living room.

A Minister of This and a Minister of That were sitting on the furniture and on the floor. There were papers, yellow notepads, and glasses of iced tea on every table. They had arrived at the US Embassy for a monthly update on the reconstruction and found no conference room was available. Our house was just around the corner, so they made a little detour.

At first it seemed like a great idea to offer the Ministry our living room as a comfortable place to work. Then I found out they were staying for lunch.

The clock was bonging 11:30. What on earth could I fix in thirty minutes for a group of men and women that ate regularly at the Polo Club? To make matter worse, the kids were going to arrive home any minute and they would be hungry.

A quick look at the inventory in the kitchen uncovered a leftover roast. The Brahma beef was always tough and chewy, but you could slice it thin enough that no one noticed—very much. There was always lots of fruit around, and deviled eggs sprinkled with paprika seemed a nice touch. I had a cook and a maid, so what could go wrong?

The maid set a loaf of bread outside in the hot sun to thaw. In my very best Spanish, I gave the cook detailed instructions to spread the roast beef as far as she could into sandwiches for the Ministry and just make peanut butter and jelly sandwiches for the kids and me. The meeting was breaking up, so I joined the group.

Everything looked wonderful. The cook had done a beautiful job of setting the table and displaying the food. As we were seating everyone, I noticed two of the men were staring at the platter of eggs. The paprika was walking around! Tiny bugs had taken up residence in the paprika can and were now on an outing on my dining room table. I scooped up the eggs and as many bugs as I could and ran for the kitchen. As I was trying to figure how to fix that problem, Al came in the kitchen carrying the artfully arranged sandwich platter.

I guess my Spanish wasn't as good as I thought. Under the fresh and crunchy lettuce and tomato was a slice of roast beef nicely nestled in a gooey bed of peanut butter and jelly.

As I was scraping and washing the peanut butter and jelly off the meat, I remember thinking that this would all seem odd if I were at home in the US. Here, it was just another day in the Foreign Service.

Life definitely got less complicated when I felt more comfortable with the language.

THE DREADFUL TERREMOTO (EARTHQUAKE)

Al's Mother came to visit. We spent a wonderful, uneventful week with her. My Mother's visit was just the opposite. She probably wondered what kind of a place we lived in. While she was visiting us we had a fire across the street in an open field. The wind was blowing our way. We were up on the roof with the hose. The fire trucks came but there was no fire hydrant. The firemen were very attentive, but could do absolutely nothing to help. They just sat there on the truck. As luck would have it, the fire did not cross the street.

A few days later, in the middle of the afternoon, we heard shots in the front yard. A guard from the bank was chasing someone through our front yard. Mother started to run to the window to see what was going on. A big mistake. I had to pull her back.

We learned from our experiences in Vietnam to go as quickly as possible in the opposite direction when there were shots or explosions. That was actually a ruse in Saigon. They would set off a little bomb, wait for the crowd to gather at the site, then set off the really big bomb. They could kill more people that way. There was no bomb that day, but when an excited, untrained guard is spraying bullets everywhere, that is not a good place to be.

A few days later Al took Jim out to teach him how to drive. The other kids went to an activity at the American School. Mother, Eric, and I were home alone. Only one of the maids was there. The house was built very deep in the lot, making it much longer than it was wide. We were in Janice's bedroom in the middle of the house. All of a sudden, we heard something that sounded like a huge freight train bearing down on us. The roar was so loud it was deafening. It took a second to realize that the windows were rattling. As the house started shaking, we ran through the hall, the den, into the informal living room, around the corner past the formal living room and out the front door. As we ran, the eight hand-carved doors lining the informal living room (which fit together with metal pegs in the ceiling and the floor), set up a terrible racket rattling against the pegs and each other. It sounded like the whole building was going to come tumbling down.

I will never forget what we saw when we reached the porch. We were out of breath and scared. The maid had reached the porch first and was already in a fetal position, crouched and huddled in a corner. I hope I never see anyone so full of terror like that ever again. She was shaking all over and literally could not speak. Her eyes were open so wide you could see the whites above and below the iris. She wouldn't—or couldn't get up. I remember Mother scooting down to put her arms around her. The poor thing just sobbed and sobbed. She had gone through the big quake the few months before and had seen several of her family members die. It must have been an absolutely horrible experience.

That earlier quake was made more terrible because it first moved either horizontal or vertical. (I can't remember which came first.) It shook everything to pieces. Huge buildings turned to rubble. Buildings had the walls fall outward and the roofs come crashing down so fast that no one could get out in time. After about twenty minutes, people started to go back into some of the buildings to check for survivors and damage. It shook a second time, but now in the opposite direction. Any breaks or weaknesses in the buildings made by the first quake now couldn't resist the movement in the opposite direction. They collapsed, trapping and killing many more people. What didn't pile up, caught fire and burned. People lived and slept outside for days after that.

There are typically no, or few, building codes in an underdeveloped country so things aren't very safe in the first place.

It took a few months, but with the buildings collapsed, the bugs didn't have anything to eat. They moved to the suburbs. We began to notice more and more bugs of every variety—as if there weren't enough bugs to begin with. People teased and said we were all members of the Bug of the Month club.

It was eerie driving through downtown. They put up barbed wire along the curbs. There was literally only one street from one side of town to the other which created quite a traffic situation. For months, a broken church tower dangled precariously over the street. Everyone picked up a little speed when driving under it. As they cleared the rubble and began to restore buildings, it was odd to go to a movie or store when it was the only building that was standing amid several blocks of rubble surrounded by barbed wire.

There were always little quakes. It was nerve-wracking because you never knew if it was going to be another "big" one. An interesting place to live ...

CALL A MARINE

Each Embassy had a contingent of Marines. Maybe because Al is an ex-marine, they were always a big part of our life. We always told the kids to call a Marine whenever possible, if they needed help. There were no police forces in most underdeveloped countries—only the national military.

Often, the social event of the year within any third-world country was the very formal Marine Corps Ball. The president of the country, the ministers, our Ambassador, and the ambassadors from most of the other countries were there. US Embassy personnel and Marines attended. Our Foreign Service officers would relieve the Marines on guard that night for a few hours so they could attend. Needless to say, security was intense. Just think what a well-placed bomb would do to that distinguished assembly.

The Marines had to raise money for the ball. They would play first-run State-side movies two or three times a week either at the Marine House where they lived or at the Embassy and charge a small sum. We went often. They were inexpensive for a family of seven and it supported the Marines. They would print up a description of the films being shown each week. However, they weren't always explicit enough and we sometimes found the kids getting a little more education than we would have liked.

Seven wives and I took cake decorating lessons each week. We hit on the idea of setting up a table at the Embassy after each class, selling the cakes, and donating the money to the Marines. It became a popular event. We did run into an unexpected problem. The fancy frosting decorations would sometimes melt in the tropical heat between the class and the Embassy. No one seemed to care.

Until Marshall Law was declared in 1975, there was a Boy Scout group. Under Marshall Law, no group was permitted to exist that wore a uniform other than the National Guard. The Scouts went underground.

The only volunteers for Scout Master were Marines. At first, we thought it was a wonderful idea. The boys could learn a lot from a Marine. Then we realized that some of what they were learning was not in the Boy Scout Manual. Overall, it was a success, but an overnight campout on the shore of Lake Jiloa was a disaster.

Jim's account: A Marine was supposed to pick us up at the Embassy. I managed to get over to the Marine House when he didn't show up. The daughter of a Department of Agriculture family was there and dropped me off at a bar where the Marine had already started his evening. He was so drunk, he couldn't drive or stay awake. He had a huge military green suburban looking thing with a stick shift. At fourteen, I had driven our station wagon a few times, but never a stick. Somehow, we managed to get back to the Marine House.

The Marine packed a box of booze and got back in the car. I drove to the campout. Once we got across the lake, he fell asleep and left a bunch of fourteen and younger boys with a big box of booze. We had to try some. Most of the kids got pretty drunk.

Several of us chopped down trees and built a big bonfire. Very late that night, someone said we needed women. We all thought that was a great idea, even though none of had any clue what we'd do once we found one. We got into the boat. About halfway across the lake the steering line for the boat broke. There we were going around in circles in the middle of the lake, drunk, and in an overloaded boat. I don't know why there wasn't a tragedy that night.

I managed to get to the motor and steer the boat back to the camp. I had to scream to get someone to shut the motor off with the key. It was turned off a little too late and we ended up quite a way up the beach, but safe. The next morning we had horrible hangovers and were stuck on the beach in a tent. We had to be rescued.

Al loved to work with wood. The Marines decided they needed a bar for the Marine House to sell beer and wine and raise money. They built a beautiful wooden bar in our garage. They had some wonderful old, old, old Marine recruiting posters and decoupaged them on the front of the bar. It was so much fun to have the young Marines hanging around the house all the time.

Holidays were sort of sad for the Marines on duty. We always filled a special dinner plate for them and took it to the Embassy on holidays. They always appreciated it and it became part of our tradition.

In a foreign country, you never left your house "alone." To a National, an American house meant there were things to steal. If we were going to be away overnight, we asked one or two Marines to stay at the house. They loved getting away from the Marine House and we felt the house was much safer. I never had the nerve to ask what they did while we were gone.

TURTLE EGGS AND HUEHUETE BEACH

When we were transferred from Washington DC to Managua, we drove and pulled a fourteen-foot travel trailer. We had to have permission from the Nicaraguense government to bring our car and the trailer into the country. After the first two weeks, when we had no stove and cooked meals in the trailer in our driveway every day, we had no particular need for it. Al made arrangements with a local co-worker to park it at his vacation house at HueHuete Beach, a short distance from Managua.

In order to reach the beach, you have to cross a river that had no bridge. Al started to pull the trailer across. The river was just wide enough and deep enough and swift enough that when both vehicles were in the water, the flow began to move the trailer downstream and drag the station wagon along with it. I can tell you, we had some anxious moments. Al somehow managed to pull forward fast enough to get to the other side with everything intact.

The scenery was a typical green, tropical landscape until we arrived at a huge craggy hill. Once beyond the hill, we were on a magnificent, pristine beach. There were a few homes with signs announcing that the beach was "privado."

The beach house where we parked the trailer was typical of the homes there. It was a cement slab with a roof. Across the back side of the slab was an enclosed bathroom and kitchen with an open-air eating area. The kitchen had huge glass windows on all four sides so you had a wonderful view of the ocean. Across the front of the slab were multiple floor-to-ceiling poles that supported numerous hammocks. There was a little area next to the hammocks that had a few chairs. That was it. What else do you really need at a beach house?

We went as often as we could. At night we would tell stories, sing, and roast marshmallows in a big fire on the sand. Al and I usually slept in the trailer. The kids thought it was more fun to sleep in the hammocks.

At certain times, turtles would lay eggs on the beach. We would go turtle-egg hunting in little Suzuki jeeps at night when the turtles came up onto the beach. Someone would sit on the hood (Yes, I know how dangerous that is.) but we were moving two miles an hour. The person on the hood would point out the turtle's trails in the sand. You had to be careful that you didn't run over them. One of our "pointers" was pretty hefty and put a big dent in the hood of one of the little jeeps. That wasn't so good.

It seemed mean to me to steal their eggs. I tried eating them, but didn't like them at all. They are pretty rubbery, but the Nicaraguense consider them quite a delicacy.

When we left Nicaragua, the Nicaraguense government wouldn't give us permission to take the trailer out of the country. We sold it to Al's co-worker and left it on the beach by his house. He never paid us, so we left the country with no trailer and no payment. We tried to take it as a casualty loss on our income tax. The IRS agent wouldn't believe our story and made us appeal it twice. They finally settled for a 50% loss. Oh well, we had a lot of fun in it while it lasted.

IGUANAS ON MY ROOF

On one of our five patios was a huge willow tree that became a highway to the roof for iguanas. When they ran, they got up on their tiptoes. When two or three ran or fought on a corrugated metal roof, the loud scratching toenails made it sound like they weighed five hundred pounds. Iguanas can grow up to a length of six feet. A huge male became a regular in our yard. He was feisty and got into one fight after another. One day we heard a tremendous racket. I ran outside. He was in a brawl on the roof. When I looked up, his tail was hanging over the eaves and down into the doorway right over my head. He looked all the world like a very large, scary dragon.

Iguanas could appear in any room of the house. I liked them around because we had bugs that showed up in droves at different times of the year. I thought they were dining on the wiggly buffet. I also thought they were eating the tarantulas that periodically appeared in the kitchen cabinets. I found out just recently that they are vegetarian and don't eat protein. I guess bugs and spiders are protein. It's probably better I didn't know that at the time.

By the way, with few or no screens, you do get accustomed to all the bugs. I remember sitting and chatting with three friends, when a dragonfly the size of a B52 bomber came in through the unscreened doorway and zoomed around the room. I don't think any of us flinched.

One of the most unusual gifts I ever received for Christmas was a dead iguana from our maid, Neela. When a Nicaraguense wanted an iguana for dinner, they would catch one by the tail, swing it around, and whop its head on the sidewalk or wall. They are considered food and we often saw this. Neela killed one for me and put it in a shoebox wrapped as a Christmas present. It was wet when I picked it up. I soon realized it was soggy with blood—or whatever it is that iguanas lose when they have their heads whacked.

We got together with a Department of Agriculture family, and had the cook prepare us a special meal of iguana stew. It was loaded with garlic and tasted terrible. None of us could eat it. It was funny to watch the kids try to feed it to the dog under the table. The dog wouldn't eat it either.

When my Mother visited, I gave her a tour of the house. Adjacent to the maid's area was a patio used for hanging laundry. The floor was unfinished concrete and had a very rough surface. An iguana fell onto the patio from a bush. Someone yelled, "iguana" and she began to run. Her rubber-soled shoes wouldn't slide over the rough floor and she tripped, falling headfirst toward the wall. When she put her hand up to stop her fall, she broke her finger. I had to rush her to a local doctor to get her finger set.

> **Lesson:** An iguana is so fast he's a blur. It's usually better to climb up on a chair or cabinet than run if you are trying to get out of its way. PS. He can–and may–climb your chair or cabinet too. I never solved that problem.

An iguana's jaws are like an alligator's. They lock. I walked into the kitchen and met one head on. Felipe got it to bite the end of a broom handle. It hung there all the while he walked through the length of the house and across the street to an open field.

Our dog, Elwood, would sometimes trap an iguana and play with it. He was bitten several times. We found one inside the house and in trying to shoo it outside, it ran into the guest bathroom which was long and deep. No one wanted to go in after it, so it stayed there a couple days. We put a sign on the door saying, "Iguana, Do Not Enter." Al finally got the idea to block all the escapes except the patio sliding door, and then turn Elwood loose. The dog lost no time in going into the bathroom and rooting it out. We all cheered him on and shooed the two of them out into the patio.

Other lizards were the geckos in the Philippines. They were small and transparent and considered good luck in the house so we left them alone. The lizards in Nigeria were about the size of the largest iguanas in Nicaragua. The male's heads were a pretty, iridescent pink/orange. We would see them on the roads and in the fields. They didn't come around the house very often.

THANKSGIVING—NICARAGUENSE STYLE

If you could find a turkey in the tropics, it was stringy and not much bigger than a large US chicken. Since Americans wanted turkey for their American holiday of Thanksgiving and often for the Christmas meal as well, the Embassy would take orders early in the summer for two turkeys. Both would be delivered sometime in November. Their reputation preceded them. Nationals knew about the plump American turkeys and would offer to purchase them for many times what they were worth.

Al always insisted that we eat every Thanksgiving meal at home. We often had guests and always took a very full plate to the Embassy for the Marine on duty. One year we received an invitation from the Embassy doctor and his wife for Thanksgiving dinner. They had included every American family in the Mission in their invitation. In addition, the doctor had just flown in from the States the day before. He invited the whole Pan Am crew to dinner. The doctor was in his early thirties with a beautiful, young wife and two young daughters. They lived in a small house on a couple of acres near kilometer twenty on the South Highway.

The plan was to have everyone bring their turkey already cooked, and some sort of a side dish or dessert. About fifteen families accepted. I decided we should go. Al wasn't happy about it, but was being a good sport.

Picnic tables were set up on the front lawn. People chose their table and set it up with their own dishes and tableware. Everyone had an assignment. It might be carving turkeys or cutting pies or setting out the salads. Carving the turkeys turned out to be a major project because the kitchen was tiny. There simply wasn't enough room for all those turkeys. Somebody set some tables on the huge, forty by forty foot covered carport next to the kitchen and the turkey carving continued outside. The huge buffet was set on more tables on the lawn. Everyone filled their plates and sat down. We said Grace and dug in.

At first there was only a sprinkle. No one minded because it was warm and that happened all the time. The sprinkle turned into a light rain. We were debating what to do when it started to pour. You never saw such scrambling as we moved the food, the full plates, and rain-soaked tables under the carport roof.

Maybe we had been in third-world countries too long, but everyone thought it was funny. We laughed and joked through the cold meal.

About six o'clock we brought out coffee and dessert. It was getting dark, so we flipped on the lights. The lights flickered and then disappeared. Lots and lots of candles came out.

While we were cleaning up, one of the men from the Pan Am crew went back to his hotel and returned with a big metal box.

Inside the box was a wooden concert marimba. He assembled it and began to play. The soft tones seemed to waft over the candlelight. Another man went home and picked up his guitar. The wife of one of the Embassy workers had an exquisite, trained, soprano voice and began to sing. It was wonderful to be sitting with friends in candlelight with the now warm, light rain pattering on the metal roof, and listening to the beautiful music.

We started to sing. We sang happy songs, and sweet songs, and silly songs, and patriotic songs, finishing with a rousing God Bless America. I don't think there was a dry eye when we finished. We all hugged each other and said good-bye. Everyone agreed it was one of the best Thanksgivings ever.

HEAD HIM OFF AT THE PASS

The X-ray technician and the local doctor said it was fine, so we did nothing, but Kenny had broken his finger. When it was still sore and bothering him, we requested that he be seen by an American doctor. We had none at the time at the Embassy. We were sent to the nearest American hospital in Panama City. Ken's friend, Geoffrey, also had a problem that needed attention. Kenny and Geoffrey, Jewell, Geoffrey's mom, and I boarded a plane for Panama and Gorgas Hospital.

We rented a car and drove to the hotel. After settling in, we decided to do some sightseeing and took the boys to see the Panama Canal. It was fascinating to see the huge doors so many stories high. Those enormous doors are supposed to be so well-balanced that a single man could open it manually. We were not fortunate enough to be there to watch a ship pass through, but they were filling one of the locks. It is an amazing sight.

The Embassy gave us instructions on how to carry a purse to prevent theft. It was especially important that day because I had both my passport and Kenny's in my purse. We carried Official passports and they were bringing many thousands of dollars on the Black Market. The Embassy taught us to carry a purse with a long shoulder strap which was thrown over your shoulder. The purse was pulled up high under your arm and you twisted your thumb through the now extra strap length letting the weight of your hand pull it down. The idea was that if someone cut the strap in the back, you still had a grip with your thumb and under your arm.

We decided it would be nice to go out and have dinner away from the hotel. For some reason, I decided to wear a sandal heel—something I rarely did. To get to our rented car, we had to walk along a narrow sidewalk that was broken hunks of cement and weeds. We were walking single file. I took up the rear. I could "feel" someone approaching from behind me and slipped over to one side as far as I could, to let them pass. I felt a sudden, hard, jerk on my purse and agonizing pain in my thumb. I turned to see a young, barefoot Panamanian man leaving in the direction we had just come in one big hurry, carrying my purse.

I yelled at the boys and Jewell. Jewell was amazing. She had worn sensible shoes and took off right behind him yelling in Spanish, "Ayudame! Ayudame! Tiene mi bolsa! (Help me, help me. He has my purse). Unfortunately, the man ran down a very long, dark alley between the many apartment buildings and Jewell followed him—a very dangerous thing to do. People started coming out onto their balconies to see what was going on. I can't remember any sudden swell of compassion from anyone, and nary a single champion came to our rescue.

I was about as much help as a sore toe. All of my Spanish vocabulary left me completely. I had the boys, so I grabbed them and tried to run down the sidewalk the way we had just come. I couldn't run in those darned shoes, so I stopped to take them off. Well, that wasn't a good plan either as I couldn't run barefoot across that jagged cement. I stopped again and put the shoes back on. The thief could have been all the way to Costa Rica by the time I got organized.

Jewell was still hot on the thief's tail and running down the alleys between the apartment buildings. The boys and I tried to "head him off at the pass." We ran down the sidewalk until we came to a break between the buildings. An American man and women were unloading groceries from the trunk of their car in a garage area. I yelled at him that the thief was heading toward him with my purse and passports.

There was a wall about five feet tall across the alley to mark off the garage area. As he turned to look in that direction, the thief came flying over the wall. The man moved directly into his path. When the thief saw he was literally running into the big American, he dropped the purse and ran. The man refused the reward I offered him.

My thumb hurt like the devil. Later, I found out it had a big crack. So much for the Embassy's theory of purse control. They needed to come up with a better idea.

The next morning we headed for Gorgas hospital. Gorgas provides care to all the military services and civilians there in the Zone. I was not expecting the acres and acres of hospital on beautiful grounds connected by many glassed-in passageways on the upper floors. What an amazing facility.

We met with the doctor. He ordered a brace that held Ken's finger in a certain position to heal properly. We were so glad that he did not have to re-break his finger.

After a very long walk, we found the prosthetic department. The doctor took the time to show us some of the wonderful artificial limbs and aids available to the unfortunate veterans who were dealing with living life minus body parts. I am sure they have come a long way from what we saw that day, but it seemed pretty spectacular at the time. It was good to know that our military had these wonderful facilities available to them.

The hospital is in the American sector called the Canal Zone. The Zone itself is pretty remarkable. The extreme contrast between Panama City and the Zone is something to see. Fourth of July Boulevard, a broad, divided byway, separates the two. As you drive down the boulevard, the view out of one side of the car is the typical dirty, poorly maintained Latin city. Apartment buildings dominate the skyline. On the other side of the car is the Zone, with manicured lawns and buildings painted bright white. There are homes, movie theaters, schools, a huge PX, bowling alleys, and little convenience stores everywhere. It is everything you would expect to find in an American city. It is hard to understand why the US just handed the Zone over to the country of Panama.

It felt good to be there—almost like being in the States. We were "starving" for good, white American bread. We stopped at a convenience store and bought a loaf of Wonder Bread. We ate nearly the whole loaf, right out of the package.

We headed to the Embassy to visit with a friend of Jewell's. She wanted to bring his two children home to visit her in Nicaragua. We had to shout over the cicadas. For just a short time, when all the maturing and mating is going on, they make a lot of racket. There are gazillions of them in every tree and all chirping at once.

At the Embassy, we met with the father of the children we were going to bring home with us. Jewell made arrangements for his wife and children to meet us at the airport. There was a young girl and boy, about ten years of age.

We boarded the Taca Airlines plane with no trouble. Everything was fine until we landed in San Jose, Costa Rica. The pilot announced that everyone had to get off the plane. Some Costa Rican big-wig wanted to use the plane for his private pleasure. Everyone got off the plane, but us.

Jewell and I decided we weren't going anywhere. We refused to get off the plane. The Captain came back and told us we had to leave. We just sat there and refused to get up. We had paid the fare back to Managua—and that is where we intended to go. They finally gave up and a group of five people boarded. They didn't look happy, but didn't say anything to us. We took off and continued on our way. I'm not sure how smart that was. We could easily have been diverted to some unwanted destination.

I remember thinking, "What else could happen on this trip?" I didn't have long to wait. When we landed in Managua and started through Customs, Jewell suddenly pushed the two visiting children behind us. The Customs agent didn't seem to notice.

When we left Customs, I asked Jewell what in the world she was doing. It turns out the kids had no entry visas to Nicaragua. We had just smuggled in two children!

Jewell's husband met us at the airport. When she told him what she had done, he erupted into a mad-man. They now had to go to the Embassy and figure out how to straighten out the mess. From what I understand, it took a lot of straightening to get it all figured out. It could have cost him his job.

What started out as a simple, quick run to Panama, turned into quite an adventure!

NOT SO PERFECT END TO A PERFECT EVENING

One night Al decided to take our kids to a movie. Jim invited a friend of his who lived in Las Bolinas, a very nice area where a lot of executives lived. The boy's father was the manager of Pan Am Airlines in Managua. When everyone arrived home, Jim's friend was with them. Everyone was all excited and talking at once.

As they turned into Las Bolinas, National Guardsmen, with weapons drawn, were crouching behind the buildings and parked cars. They stopped the car. They waved Al off and wouldn't let him pass. Al drove a short distance to a restaurant and called the Embassy to find out what was happening.

There had been a party that evening at the home of the Minister of Agriculture. It was across the street from the home of Jim's friend. Many dignitaries and executives were in attendance. Our US Ambassador Shelton made an appearance at the function. A group of terrorists had broken into the house. The Minister and three guards were killed. They were holding everyone else hostage. The National Guard had been called in and had surrounded the house. Everyone thought our Ambassador was still inside and was also being held. Al and the kids had driven into a very dangerous situation.

After Al dropped off everyone at our house, he went to the Embassy to get an update. He said it looked like an arsenal. The Marines were ready for whatever came next. While Al was there, a message came from the Ambassador saying he was safe. He had left the party about twenty minutes before the break-in. Needless to say, it changed the situation for us considerably. Everyone breathed a little easier. Thankfully, Jim's friend had a phone at home. Al called his parents from the Embassy to tell them we would keep their son as long as was needed. It was to be several days.

The terrorists were demanding a huge sum of money in American dollars and that fourteen prisoners be released. It took several days of negotiations. To gather the ransom money, every bank in Managua was drained of American dollars. For weeks afterward, if you needed American dollars, you were out of luck. The terrorists also wanted safe transportation by air out of the country. A day and time was set. Buses would pick up everyone at the Las Bolinas house and drive them to the airport. The hostages would be left on the buses. The terrorists would board a plane parked on an isolated tarmac at the airport. The exact day and time were kept secret

At the appointed time, the hostages and terrorists were loaded into two buses. They set out for the airport with military escorts in front and the rear. The earthquake damage was still everywhere so there was still only one road open through the whole of downtown. The airport was just on the other side.

On the same day, Al had to go to the airport on Official business. He drove to the Embassy to ask if it was safe. He was assured that it would be fine. As he was driving and nearing the airport, he suddenly realized he was between two buses—buses loaded with hostages and terrorists. To this day he isn't sure how, but he was right in the middle of the terrorist convoy.

There was only one road, and no way to get out of the predicament. He was afraid that if he tried to pass, they would mistake him for someone trying to interfere and would shoot him. He decided to stay right where he was. Al said everyone on the buses was watching him. Why the terrorists didn't do something is anybody's guess. Eventually, the buses turned off into a guarded entrance to the airport.

When he got home he had quite a story to tell—and he was furious. He immediately went marching over to the Embassy and told them what had happened and how close they had come to getting him killed. He still gets mad when he talks about it.

Martial Law was declared soon after.

> **From Jim:** Janice and I encountered a similar hostage situation. We were at a party at the home of an Ambassador. I was going to drive a boy home. When we got to the entrance of the residential area of Las Colinas, there were National Guard all over. A machine gun was mounted on top of one of the cars. They swung the gun around and pointed it at us. Four or five men came running toward us, waving their weapons and waving us away. I gunned it, spun some dirt up, and high-tailed it out of there. The boy stayed the next couple days with us.

SO MANY VOLCANOES

There were volcanoes nearby at each of our Posts. We traveled to see Mayon Volcano in the Philippines. Some say it is the eighth wonder of the world. Mayon reaches over eight thousand feet. It is said to be one of the most beautiful volcanic cones in the world. It is visible for miles. The volcano is still active. It erupted in 2000 and 2001.

We also visited Taal in Tagaytay. Taal blew its top off years before and now there is a lake in the middle of the crater. It was so darned hot you couldn't breathe the day were there. We didn't know that the reason it was so hot was because it was going to explode in a matter of days. Glad we missed the occasion.

In Nicaragua, there was a large, active volcano in the middle of Lake Managua. It stayed quiet while we were there. Jiloa Volcano in Managua was similar to Taal with a lake in the cone.

I was very excited when we took my Mother to visit Costa Rica because we were going to the top of Mount Irazu, another active volcano called "the Powder Keg of Nature." We drove around and around the mountain to the peak at eleven thousand feet. The curves were so tight on the narrow road that we lost a hubcap. As far as I know, it is still up there.

What a disappointment. The crater was supposed to have water in it. All I could see was one huge, flat area—not too far down—that looked like a moonscape. We were so high that we were in clouds. It was like looking through a dense fog. Maybe I missed something.

I do remember the effect of the altitude. We all felt light-headed. It was hard to get our equilibrium when we tried to walk. They advised us to walk very, very slowly.

But then! A relatively small volcano near Managua started to act up. Our friend, George, found a four-wheel drive jeep somewhere. We piled his kids and mine into it and set off for the volcano.

The mountain wasn't much more than a good-sized hill, but the dirt was so loose near the peak that we kept sliding backwards (no road, of course). George got us up there. We found an area on the undefined ridge consisting of a large slab of rock and no loose dirt. We certainly didn't want anyone to fall in. Everyone had to lie down flat, work their way on their belly to the edge, and then peer over.

It was fascinating to me and I think, to everyone. The molten lava was moving like ocean waves on a rough sea. It would burst here and there spewing up in your direction, throwing off little bits of molten lava. Every minute or so, a huge pillar of red, hot lava would come way, way up and then slide back down. None of this reached a point anywhere near the top where we were, but it wasn't that far down either. It was just right for a spectacular show.

From Janice: I remember crawling on my belly out on that rock and watching the lava that looked so much like the ocean. It was beautiful! I remember that we left at sunset. Anyone who has been that close to the equator knows how spectacular the sunsets are. When the sun starts to set, the mountains all around become black against the bright orange sky. There were dozens of bright green parrots flying all over the sky. The colors were magnificent. I'll never forget that day—one of my favorites.

From Jim: I was friends with a boy from school whose father was a volcanologist. A friend of theirs came to Managua for field tests. At school, he asked if anyone wanted to go to the volcano. I went.

We drove to a small volcano, eight hundred to nine hundred feet, called Cerro Negro. We had to hike several miles over fresh lava. By the time we got there, my tennis shoes were so shot and worn through from that short hike that I couldn't stand the heat on my feet. The men used sleds and slid to the bottom while we waited. They took their measurements and climbed back up. There was so much ash that every three steps up, we fell back two. We jumped out as far as we could and sank to our waists when we landed.

The other volcano was Mombo Tombo. Someone said it was the most perfect cone in the world. One other thing I remember was flying to Florida. I flew on Taca Airlines to El Salvador. The trip went right over the top of at least twenty volcanoes in the "ring of fire." You really didn't get a sense of what a "ring of fire" was until you flew over it.

A BIG MISTAKE

Al and I ran some errands late one afternoon, leaving the kids at home with the maids. Seventeen-year-old Jim was in charge. We arrived home to learn that he had driven away with some friends.

Hours passed and we heard nothing. We had no phone, so Al got in the car and drove to the friend's' home. Their parents were frantic too. The two fathers drove around to likely places, with no luck. They finally went to the Embassy to report them missing. There is no friendly policeman to call in most third-world countries, only the military. The good Lord was shining down on us because Gunter, the US advisor to the Nicaraguense National Guard, was still in-country and could help us. Forty-eight hours later, we would have had no help. Gunter left Nicaragua for good.

Completely exhausted, Al dragged in after daylight. He was furious. He told me the boys were arrested on the charge of possession of marijuana and that Jim could rot in jail. He left me standing in the middle of the kitchen and went to bed.

Al hated drugs. He always told the kids that if they chose that route, they were on their own. Now, we were facing that decision head-on. Even if we chose to fight, drugs is the only area of the law where the Embassy has absolutely no jurisdiction, so our chances of getting Jim out of trouble were slim to none.

This ordeal is best told by Jim. Here is his account:

> This is a story that I am convinced God had His hands on. I wanted to go to military school. I was nearly finished with admission requirements to Annapolis and wanted to be a submariner. God had other plans.
>
> In the early afternoon, some friends came by our house. The father of two of the boys was the General Manager of the

Standard Oil refinery, the only oil refinery in the country. The father of another boy ran the Department of Electric Power, Enaluf. The fourth boy was from the States and was visiting the son of the Foreign Minister.

On the way to our house, the boys stopped by a park downtown and bought a small quantity of pot. A Colonel in the National Guard with two squad cars spotted them at the park and followed them. He let them come to our door and pick me up. The Colonel decided that our house was the "pusher" house and that he had hit the jackpot.

I had no idea where they had been. I thought we were just going for a ride. I didn't think I would be gone very long so I got in their car with no shirt or shoes. We went only one block when the boy driving saw the National Guard cars behind us. He grabbed something and threw it out the window.

The squad cars stopped us and made us get out of our car. They said they smelled pot on our breath and searched the car. No one had smoked anything, so there was nothing on anyone's breath. There was no pot to find.

Dad always told me to say, "Lleveme a la Embajada Americana," which means, "Take me to the American Embassy." We were so close to the Embassy I could see it, but the Colonel would have none of it. I was so scared I just kept repeating the phrase over and over. The Colonel pulled his gun, shoved me in the back seat of the squad car, and shut the door. The boy from the States was put in the car with me. The other two boys drove their car with two officers in the back seat. I was told later they had been stopped before and could always give the officers their pot or some money and they would be released. But the Colonel was with them that day ...

We were driven to jail. We were not allowed a phone call and they took everything we had; our money, our identification, everything in our pockets. The jail was a large, open prefab metal warehouse on a slab. Inside were some offices in a corner, a small six-by-six holding cell, and two larger cells on either side. The cells were like zoo lion's cages with black metal bars. The top was about twelve feet high and there were two-by-twelve planks lined up so a guard with a M1 rifle could pace back and forth.

Men were held on one side. The other side was divided by a wall for men and women. About fifty beds were pushed together, three bunks high with no bedding. There were twice as many people as bunks. There was a row of open bathrooms behind a wall with no seats. None of the guards would go inside the dirty cells, so a prisoner with an attitude problem was in charge.

The first night, six of us were crammed into the holding cell. There was only room for one person to lie down so we took turns for an hour or two at a time. One of the boys loaned me his shirt when it was my turn. A man gave us cigarettes to smoke.

The next morning, they split us up; two of us on one side, two of us on the other. I was with the boy from the States who spoke no Spanish. I spoke very little.

While we were there, someone was beaten and bloodied by the inmate guard. We just shut up and laid low. A woman across the way was in labor for hours and hours. She screamed every few minutes with contractions. We met a man who had been there for two months who was supposed to be there overnight for drunkenness. There were killers, rapists, political prisoners—you name it. There were men sleeping together too.

I slept during the day. It was the only time a bunk was available. At night, I slept across the middle of two bunks with the center digging into my back. I was a gringo. I got last pick.

I thought we reached Dad by wrapping a note around a rock that said, "Call the American Embassy and tell them there are four Americans in jail." We threw it to a lady out the window. By that time though, Gunter may have found us as well. In any case, Dad showed up the next morning.

I didn't eat until the fourth and last day. I finally tasted a piece of tortilla that morning. By that time, I really didn't care and wanted to die. The cook was an old, fat, dirty woman with a big stir-stick in a huge cauldron over an open fire. There were dogs running around just outside the warehouse. I was afraid I was going to die or have dysentery if I ate anything. Most of time, I just sat around and stared out the window.

The most difficult moment of the whole ordeal was on the third morning. Dad appeared with a shirt, some socks, and some shoes (thank God), and all he had time to tell me was "Son, I don't know what I'm going to do." That was it. After that, I thought I was in there for good.

On the fourth day, they told us we were going to have pictures taken. They took us into a room and there were all our fathers. They read aloud part of a so-called law book. They admitted they had nothing on me and said they'd been watching the other boys. I left that room and never saw any of them again.

Dad took me straight to the barber shop and had my head shaved. Then we went to the Residence and I told Ambassador Shelton my story. The only school that had accepted me at the time was Bellarmine, a Jesuit school in California—so that's where I went. The very next morning, I got on a plane and didn't see my family for a long time. It wasn't until the second Christmas that we decided it would be safe to return.

Instead of becoming a war-monger, I ended up a peace-loving Christian.

Our Managua House

Al had to make furniture

Trapped iguana

600 square blocks of damage

Rubble

Clearing the Rubble

WE WENT BACK HOME

July 1976

THE END OF THE STORY

Jim's incident with the Nicaraguense National Guard set a whole series of events into motion. We now had Butch in college and Jim in high school in the States. It also led to Janice leaving for high school in the US. That made three of the five children away from home. This factor, added to some important others, led to Al's resignation in 1976.

Jim was at Bellarmine, an excellent Jesuit school that accepts boarding students. It was just blocks away from my Mother. We felt there was a greater chance for discipline in a religious environment. Study was definitely stressed at the school, but Jim was a good student so we were not worried about that. He graduated with a 4.0 grade average.

He seemed to like the priests and they seemed to like him. We did wonder about a few things. Mostly kid stuff. His graduation picture shows that he had no use for barbershops. We heard that he wore hiking boots to the graduation dance. Can't remember all the circumstances now, but he somehow ended up with our brand new Ford Granada for a week or so. He decided to take a little trip to Oregon—without asking us.

Jim kept having short periods where he would black out and not remember anything. We thought it might be drugs. Or maybe a bang on the head while playing football. When we were on home-leave, we took him to the Stanford University Hospital. They were interested in him because they were in the midst of a study of Narcolepsy and thought that might be Jim's problem.

Narcolepsy allows a person to function as though awake, but they are actually asleep and don't remember what they are doing. Jim would walk in his sleep when he was very young and this could have been related. None of the tests were conclusive. I guess we will never know what it was. It eventually disappeared.

In Nicaragua, when Jim came home to visit, he talked and talked about his school. Janice decided it sounded so good, she wanted to go to the States too. It was a huge decision, but she wanted very much to go. Not only did we have her welfare to worry about, but we knew that if she left home for high school that we would probably end the Department of State career as well. We did not want three of our five children somewhere other than home.

Sacred Heart is a Catholic girl's school in Menlo Park, California, run by nuns. Janice was not happy there. I'm not sure what she was doing, but a nun told me she was a "foot stomper." She buddied around mostly with the Latin girls instead of the US girls. Either my Mother would pick her up, or she would ride the train to San Jose to visit. Mother wrote often and kept us up on the news. Both Bellarmine and Sacred Heart would call her with questions. Thinking of it now, it was too much to ask of her. She was always so willing to help.

Butch had transferred to San Jose State. I don't know how much contact he had with his grandmother. He adopted Toni's (his future wife) family and spent his time with them.

I always regretted the day I first let him fly off to California by himself for college. He was only sixteen. Al insisted that California Lutheran (Al's alma mater), was the only place for him to be. He could have stayed with us for at least another year on the East coast. We had little money to send him. I know that made it very hard. I thank God he found Toni and her family—and they took him in. I will always feel bad that he had to find a substitute family to take our place.

All the kids were ahead of themselves academically and socially. It made them very young to be on their own, even though they were high school or college students. We went back to the States to be near them.

As you think back on your decisions, they seem logical at the time. Given the exact same set of circumstances, you would probably make the same decision again. All of our children became wonderful, responsible adults, so maybe the overseas experience was okay. I guess I will never know if living in third-world countries hurt them or helped them. In any case, by being exposed to all these cultures, they now have a yardstick with which to measure the United States. I think it created an appreciation of what we have here, and hopefully, made them better citizens of this country and the world.

Al may not have met his original goal to save the people of Mexico, but I know there were citizens of Vietnam, Nigeria, Bangladesh, and Nicaragua that were glad he was there.

As for me, I discovered a world I would never have known if I had stayed in my cocoon in Small Town, USA. I learned that important events are occurring all over this globe that affect not only the people in a given country, but simultaneously, the lives of people in many countries, including the United States.

I saw life without freedom. The fragile freedoms we enjoy here were won and are being preserved with the sweat and blood of our men and women. It is important to support them and to be aware of events at home and around the world. Apathy is an enemy.

Racial prejudice might disappear if we didn't teach our children to hate. We found wonderful friends in many cultures.

People in high positions are to be respected, maybe admired, maybe even feared, but not held in awe. They are only human beings. The Lord will decide how well they use their power.

And finally, set goals and plan ahead, but take life one day at a time. My secret: You can do almost anything for one day.

ABOUT THE AUTHOR

Nancy Stone lived a challenging eight years in developing countries. Back in the United States, she founded a bookkeeping service that led to a second career as Vice President of Operations in a business data disaster-recovery company. She and her husband are retired and live in New Mexico.